YOU ARE YOUR
BRAND

BUILDING

FROM

THE

INSIDE

OUT

FELICIA *R* SHAKESPEARE

I dedicate this book to the individuals in my life who believe in me with an unwavering resolve. Your prayers, your words or merely your presence, have been my wind. The two words I use with deepest gratitude are, thank you. I love you all.

"Nothing I've done in life I've done on my own."
—AUTHOR UNKNOWN

FOREWORD
By Dr. Willie Jolley
Best Selling Author and #1 Inspiration Speaker in America

To be or not to be …that is the question! Once upon a time there was a great writer named William Shakespeare who compelled his reader to look at life from a different perspective. Today we have a new writer who has the last name of Shakespeare, who is also compelling readers to think bigger and bolder. The difference is that William Shakespeare was a man in the middle centuries; this Shakespeare is a woman who is making exciting things happen today!

When I met Felicia Shakespeare I was impressed with her enthusiasm and commitment to positively impact people with her word, both written and spoken. I was also impressed with her commitment to helping people to see the power of their brands in building their success, both personally and professionally.

Over the years I have constantly been focused on "Building My Brand" and I have worked hard to build it in everything I do. I wanted to build a brand that would help people to do more, be more and achieve more. I wanted to build a brand to empower people globally to use their faith to live their best lives. I started by first by getting focused on inspirational speaking, then added motivational music, then added books, then radio, then television, then live stage events, then internet and social media, then digital messaging and speaking. The challenge was that I did it intuitively and could not articulate systematically how I did it. When I met Felicia Shakespeare I met someone who was able to help people get a system to build a powerful brand.

The purpose of this book is to share what Felicia learned through her own experiences as a business and education professional. She can provide information that will help you understand the concept of personal branding. After reading this book you will be able to identify what brand you want to portray and move forward with delving into the work that will develop and define your "brand", "mark", "signature", "imprint" that coincides with *your* vision of how you see yourself and how you ultimately want to be seen by others. Felicia›s insight will help others avoid the traps and pitfalls that can lead to negative branding because it's much easier to build a positive brand than it is to nullify a negative brand. *You Are Your Brand* is written for a wide audience, which is why she uses examples from all walks of life. It's written for the entrepreneur who is just starting up a company. It's written for the person just starting their first job. It's written for the seasoned veteran who has been on the same job for several years, holding the same position, have not been promoted and does not understand why. It's written for the college aged student who may or may not be involved in social media but needs to understand the ramifications of sharing personal information, texts and photos through the various social media outlets, their digital footprint. It's written for anyone who wants to grow a powerful personal brand!

I recommend you read this book, then re-read it, then share it with your friends. It will help you to do more, be more and achieve more!

Contents

INTRODUCTION

No one told me the truth. No one prepared me on how to hit the ground running and scramble my way to success. That is, until I landed face-first into a brick wall named Doreen Dukes. I was 18 at the time, had landed my first job at a local bank, and thought I was doing fairly well. The day that she tipped me off to one major fact of life was an eyebrow-raising experience that has been etched in my memory for more than 2 decades. Sitting at my spot in the drive-up window, a call came through, and I answered the phone with a simple word *plaza* which I thought designated the branch I worked in.

Doreen, a woman with alabaster skin and a no-nonsense attitude, was on the other end of that call and gave me the scolding of my life. "You don't answer the phone like that. You say, 'Hello, thank you for calling the Bank of . . . My name is Felicia Shakespeare. How may I assist you?' This isn't your house; this is a place of business."

The moment I was mature enough to understand what a *brand* really meant was on the heels of this one woman explaining that I was representing the bank, *not* Felicia Shakespeare. They had an image to uphold, and I was supposed to be an extension of that image. Unfortunately, prior to this incident, all I understood about life was that I was supposed to be most pleasant and punctual, then I would reap the benefits of the kind of life others only dreamed about. No one had explained some of the simpler facts of life that would take me a lot further in the business world by helping me to understand my *personal brand*, as it relates to *corporate brand* and maneuvering in real-life interactions.

Everyone is familiar with brands on a corporate level since we encounter them on a regular basis, through print, commercial, and social media, as well as in day-to-day experiences. McDonald's, Burger King, and White Castle are a minor example of easily recognizable brands that are encountered more often than others. Each is known for having a particular taste, style, look, feel, smell, and has spent millions of dollars on advertising to further the positive outreach of that brand. Well, in some cases, a little negative branding has slipped in no matter how much money they've thrown around.

Take White Castle, for instance. Though it brings to mind that small white carton with a blue castle etched on the front, in certain circles, another not-quite-pleasant imagery comes to mind that I'm certain that company did not anticipate along the way. I don't have to spell it out because you know *exactly* what I'm talking about—and mentioning it can bring a few laughs as well. Still, no *negative* imagery of White Castle's main product *sliders* has tarnished their brand in such a way that it has impacted its ongoing success. And that's because there is such a solid footing with the brand they've established, and they can take the hit from a few laughs because people, despite their reservations on that one issue, keep buying them by the sackfuls.

Businesses can recover from unanticipated negative backlash. People, not so much. Which is why I found it necessary to pen a book about *personal branding* and how to build a brand from the inside out. People rarely see themselves as a brand and that who they are has everything to do with how others formulate one word to represent what they envision of you: powerful, dynamic, awesome, inspiring, strong, and courageous. On the flip side, there's uncommitted, unassuming, negative, and weak, along with a whole host of other adjectives to choose from.

Dr. Rebecca Sherrick, the president of a university I attended, tipped me off to something that was becoming a major issue of concern. Many young women and men exiting college are lacking the elements needed to formulate a personal brand that would make them successful in the careers they've prepared for. The younger ones seem to have no concept of punctuality, follow-up, how to pen a proper letter or e-mail, let alone loyalty to a new job. The conversation came about after I'd made arrangements to meet and reconnect several years later in order to gain a pulse on the current state of higher learning institutions. What better place to start than my alma mater. I had met Dr. Sherrick some years earlier when she personally presented me with the Shining Example teaching award. I knew she would give me the truth with her no-nonsense style. Because of her formal education and many years on the higher education circuit, I knew she would be a great resource for me to really gain a pulse of the state of affairs in this particular segment of education. Over the years, many experiences would come into my life to trigger my interest in this aspect of branding, the personal brand.

When I began writing about the topic of personal branding, I initially thought of the technique which can be traced back to ancient times. The method used to identify and separate livestock from one another, known as *hot branding*, included the use of a branding iron rod (imagine a metal stick) which was placed in a fire and heated until the iron would glow at the tip's end. The end of the iron rod had been formed into a unique symbol, or mark, belonging to the owner. This symbol or mark was then stamped onto the livestock's hide so there would be no mistake where, and to whom, the animal belonged.

The concept or purpose for branding in this context was quite simple. In those times when owning livestock was a potent source of income, there were limited designated areas of land available for grazing, which meant livestock for all ranchers were forced to graze together. The owners had no other means to identify their own livestock other than through the *roundup*. The symbol that had been placed on an animal helped the rancher identify his own, along with the documents to prove that ownership when asked at certain checkpoints.

Believe it or not, branding animals is still something that is done in this day and age. Now, the use of microchips and identification numbers exist to achieve this end. Because there's nothing new under the sun, we use the same concept or connector in our world today to identify a brand for a person or a business. The identification via symbols (i.e., logos, phrases, taglines, etc.) and other forms of representation is what people use today to represent their uniqueness in their world. However, a good majority of people focus on the external means of creating a brand. Many fail to realize that your brand starts with who you are, where you're from, and what roads you take to reach the level of success that you feel is within your reach. Branding, as we know it, is for the purpose of clear identification and ownership. People want to "stand out" as being a distinct original. Our symbols, words, behavior, and methods not only identify who we are but how we market who we are.

Most entities that are serious about legitimizing their brand begin with a number of different ways to preserve and legalize aspects of their brand identity. Whether corporate or individual, using a trademark or copyrighting is an important aspect of protecting what belongs to your brand.

On a corporate and business level, branding is an easier undertaking these days, but what about those who wish to do it on a personal level, which, I might add, is more important than any other branding module I can think of. *Your* brand is the first thing that greets people on the job, at church, at home, in social settings, and if your brand has not been developed in such a way that promotes, positions, and propels, you'll be making an impression that far outlasts what you'd hoped for.

What makes you up as a brand? What experiences have formed your brand? What measures have you taken to protect your brand?

These questions and many others are what drove me to write this book, and it is my hope that something between these pages will help you identify:

- **Power**

- **Purpose**

- **Potential**

Yes, there are many books on branding in the industry, but I haven't found many that deal with personal branding in such a way that focuses on internal development. Here is my opportunity to share what I've learned, and if you're reading this book, you are bound for an *inside* makeover.

1
WHAT IS A BRAND, REALLY?

rand or branding seem to be a part of the latest lingo. Almost every time I watch television, read something online, or attend a workshop or training session, someone is consistently referencing themselves, or something connected to them, as part of a brand. Whether referring to a business or a person, the term *brand* can have a variety of meanings within very different scenarios. The scope or range of brand reference comes from celebrities in their own right as well as from everyday people. In almost every age group and industry, discussions of being a *brand* seem to be the latest of hot topics.

What is a brand? I've already walked through examples of what the word means in terms of identification of product as it directly relates to terms that focus on *sales* and *marketing*. The best business leaders consider these methods to be critical components in order for them to capitalize on promoting products and services. In most instances, how well this plan is implemented determines if a single product will ever make it into the hands of the general public. A great marketing campaign that signifies one's brand is most critical to the success of any personal or business growth.

Personal Brand Defined

Recently, a friend shared something profound with me about this topic. A movie she had seen starring actress Jacqueline Bisset as Madame Simone and Linda Hamilton as Joanna Scott, has impacted the way she organizes her life. In the movie, Joanna, whose life is in flux due to a husband who has left her for a younger woman, is set to be *set up* by Madame Simone, who is a matchmaker to millionaires. Simone grooms young women for marriage by putting them through etiquette courses and other experiences that give them the foundation for being a good wife before pairing them with a husband who is extremely wealthy. Simone chooses whether she will take on a young woman as a client by first having her empty out whatever purse she's carrying. The items which are spread out on a table are the deciding factor. If the items are messy, or if the purse contains crumbled up pieces of papers, or other things that should have been long-ago discarded, or if, in fact, there is entirely too much in the purse altogether, the woman is dismissed immediately. No conversation needed, no explanations given, no second chances—just take the items, your purse, and yourself out the front door and miss the opportunity of a lifetime.

The message was plainly conveyed that for a woman lining herself up to be a mate/wife to a man who already has his life together on so many levels—then you should too. To this day, my friend only keeps a few items in her purse—keys, wallet, a small bottle of perfume, breath mints, a pen, her cell, and a tiny container of lotion. Not because she wishes to marry a millionaire (she'd rather make her own millions and have a mate appreciate the other aspects of who she is according to her), but that one scene in the movie showing it as a deciding factor in the fate of someone's life was equally as impactful as the scolding I received from Doreen Dukes that day at the bank. Personal brand can be determined by the smallest of things—and in this case, it was being organized and being prepared.

My friend also takes the same approach in other aspects of her life. She organizes her finances, her home, her car, her desk at work, and projects quite the same way as she does her purse—all the result of watching a movie for entertainment purposes. Additionally, it's also how she chooses clients for editing projects for her editing business by asking to see their media kit, Web site, social media page, personal recommendation from a reliable source, then having a conversation that poses several questions related to their goals. Every element is a different key to that potential client's personal branding and whether it's worth putting in her valuable time to develop them into national best-selling authors.

Let's start right now with the aspect of what it means to be a *personal brand*. Personal branding is when an individual, instead of a business or entity, is the focus of the brand. A personal brand, in its true essence, is the way one represents himself or herself in and to the world. Though what people recognize most is the type of branding that applies to a business or entity, this book will focus on the personal side, which is the *inside*. The perception of how we establish ourselves in any situation as individuals represents who we are to the world and how we are received by society as a whole. These factors: character development, integrity, and knowing your purpose are only a few of the factors that constitute the creation of a personal brand.

The most suitable definition I can give for the purpose of this book is that a personal brand, defined in this context, is how you are distinguished, categorized, or perceived by people around you and the world at large. Who you are at all times will parlay into your personal, professional, and business brand. You are the reason that a brand even exists in any of these situations. In other words, you, the individual or entity, can be viewed as the actual "product."

So, this question begs an answer . . . At this moment in time, if you had to sum "your brand" up in a word, what would it be?

2

BE YOUR BRAND ON PURPOSE: BRAND INTENTIONALITY

Everyone possesses a particular talent, skill, or ability, and sometimes more than one simultaneously, identifying as a "brand." Michael Jordan, Steve Jobs, Joel Osteen, Iyanla Vanzant, and Richard Branson all bring a particular brand to mind when their names, images, or even the companies they represent flash before our eyes.

Michael Jordan, easily distinguishable from others in the basketball industry, was one of the first to, in such a way that excelled, dominated, and commanded our attention in the sport. His personal brand, however, took a hit when perceived as a silo player, and only when Phil Jackson, his coach at the time, explained that in order to become a winner, his personal brand would have to be intertwined with that of a team. Notice that at a certain period of time, even though Michael was the focal point, no matter what members made up that team, they hit that championship circle six times. He, along

with each member of the team, became synonymous with the word—
winner. Why? Because early on, someone he trusted explained to him
the importance of changing his brand to achieve his ultimate goal. On
another note, that part of his brand was what people like to remember most, and it far outweighed any negative accusations about this
phenomenal basketball star. Behavior is also very much part of personal branding and people tend to forget that. People truly take note
more of what we *do* and much less of what we say.

Take an elementary school teacher for instance; one that is presented with a new class of students at the beginning of the year. By the
end of the week, she or he's already figured out the troublemakers, the
teacher's pet, the class helpers, the most dependable, and the attention
starved, simply by their actions and behaviors. The teacher might use
that type of branding (fairly or unfairly) in their approach to deal with
issues that arise within the scope of the day. The same holds true for
how people gauge your brand—first impressions of you, your behavior, your actions, and your "presence" can open a door or opportunity,
or it can slam it shut without you even knowing the effects.

Simply seeking a way to offer those talents and/or skills that you've
developed in your own unique way is a form of branding that takes
tenacity, courage, and consistency. Branding is a way to also display
how you are unique with your abilities, and in many cases, can be
identifiable as one's *calling*. In this instance, it's important to identify
when the need for your particular brand is "in season" so momentum
or movement at that time is not lost.

If you've ever had an "aha!" moment, or a series of them, they are
life-changing in the fact that they are pivotal eye-openers. Finding
your purpose can be considered equivalent to that. Oprah is a great
example of that. I love her quote:

> *I believe there's a calling for all of us. I know that every
> human being has value and purpose. The real work of*

*our lives is to become aware. And awakened. To answer
the call. It's not that I've always known what I would be.
It was just clear to me at an early age who I wouldn't be."*
(www.oprah.com/spirit)

Many would dare to say that their calling equates to their very purpose in life. I would further define calling as the *ability* or something that you are capable of doing very well without much effort.

When you, as an individual or an entity, begin to recognize your own personal impact on any part of living, it is important to see your value and to embrace the lessons with each experience in life to achieve higher levels of success and explore even greater potential that lies inside of you. This is not intended to be just for the sake of a goal or for the purpose of gaining notoriety, but essentially the mission is for one to reach a level of knowing that you are living up to the potential of your life's purpose. Tangible opportunities will present themselves to show your best "you" which is part of your reason for even being. The intention becomes not just the focus of where you're going during the process, but more importantly, on *who* you are becoming.

You Won't Know Your Brand if You Don't Know Your Purpose . . .

Individuals who gain any type of notoriety in their lives, careers, or business tend to have a clearer scope of what they want their brand to represent. They tend to have a better handle on their goals and mission. Why? Because they have a *purpose.*

My organized friend that I spoke of earlier has a son who stumbled on the way to learning his purpose at one point in his life. He was brilliant, creative, and was certain to be the type of young man who excelled in anything he put his mind to. He hit a rough patch during puberty that carried all the way to his sophomore year in high school.

Throughout those years, he went from being a straight-*A* student to hitting *D*s and *F*s in subjects that were once considered his favorite. My friend took it personally as a parent that maybe she wasn't doing enough. Tutoring, changing schools, punishments, taking away privileges—none of it served the purpose of snapping him back on the trajectory he had been before.

Then she switched him to a school that began to put the word *scholar* in front of his name instead of student, which caused a minor shift. This action was followed by taking him on a college tour where he was able to see the "end result" of all the classes, studying, and learning he'd been into all those years. This created a major shift in his thinking because he saw the goal—the "finish line" and realized exactly what he had to do to walk across to the "finish line." Suddenly, those former *D*s and *F*s became *A*s and *B*s, and class assignments and projects were given full-blown attention. Not only did he graduate, but he was given a presidential scholarship to the university he most wanted to attend. He had reached within himself and applied the strength, balance, and focus so that he didn't buy into a "failure" brand completely. That's when things fell into place.

Usually when a person begins to clearly position themselves as a brand, they have come to realize that whether through their own instincts or through much counsel from others that maybe, just maybe, they are "on to something." There are moments when we receive a revelation or understanding and are enlightened in a way that we had not been before that point in time. In the case of the young man in the previous paragraphs, his revelation was shifted between being labeled a "scholar" and then a college tour that gave him another set of goals. At the point of clear positioning and understanding in most people's lives, it would be in their interest to capitalize on that "something." Expressions like the terms *ride the wave* or *when you're hot you're hot* best fit this scenario. The most wonderful times in life are when the "light comes on" in an area that was once dark to you.

Seemingly, what could be considered a "moment of truth" in your life is literally when *your purpose* has been revealed in such a way that it can't be ignored. You'll begin to see a way to achieve something in your life that maybe you could not previously envision. The path that can get you there is now clear, whereas the moment before, everything was not so obvious. Sometimes this is the point where it's necessary or critical to solicit counsel from those who may be more equipped in an area than you are; an expert of sorts. Experts are critical to enhancement or further development of various aspects of our life's journey. Sometimes, it may be necessary to seek out this type of support from outside of our immediate circle; a definite way to keep up the momentum.

Depending on what has been identified as your purpose or calling, opportunities to grow will become more identifiable. Suddenly, you'll be at a random meeting and a particular piece of information comes up that has nothing to do with the meeting, but everything to do with an opportunity that will further one of your goals. You hear it clearly because you're tuned in, whereas everyone else at the table might frown and wonder: where did that come from? On another note, there might be a song or writings in a book, something out of the blue that has a message that is a guideline to your next steps toward success. Though you might have heard that piece or read the passage before, suddenly, you're able to pick up on the message and know that there are action steps you must now take.

You must be willing to make the necessary steps or changes to get to your desired destination in life. When you have prepared yourself, your identity, brand, and area of expertise now begin to shine through! Whether you choose to take on or create new opportunities—great or small—to expose your talent, market products, or services you've created, opportunities now become limitless! Whatever direction you take to increase your capacity or your reach, the time to do it is when you've clearly identified purpose. Taking the steps is when you're the most likely to reach your goals!

Planning Is Key . . .

The first key step to any endeavor is planning. Mapping out a direct plan of action in which key goals are identified is critical to your success. Lacking a plan of action can be detrimental to your progress and possibly cause major setbacks if pursued out of a proper sequence and level of preparedness. Take, for instance, those who desire to play the lottery. You're sitting in front of the television watching the official pull number after number from the machine. Your shoulders are tense with anticipation as you check off digits that are familiar to you. On each one, your breath hitches and heart rate speeds up—all six, seven, eight numbers match what you've had in mind, right? Unfortunately, you didn't take that trip to the store and actually play, and yet, you're sitting there expecting to win. It sounds illogical, right? I'm not promoting gambling but the idea of the ability to execute. If you don't have the ability to follow through, you will remain in a "what could have been" state of mind.

Let's take it from another angle. Many have made millions in one year and are deep in debt the next. The opportunity is there, they've made all the right moves, but their mind-set, their brands, and their lives are still positioned to remain at their current status. So because they weren't prepared, the tide of prosperity rolled in, and it rolled right back out, leaving them in worse shape than when they started. Have you ever noticed that the media announces that there's been a winner of a substantial amount of money, and it takes days, sometimes weeks or months, for them to come forward? Those winners are putting a plan in place before they accept that money—debt payoffs, trust funds, and estate plans, preparing to close their circle of friends and family, laying out exactly what to do with the cash and when. Why? So they won't fall into the same category as those others I mentioned—back to square one and in debt. Whether it be a cash fall from any unexpected source, there must be a plan put in place in order to thrive in any type of life-altering circumstance.

Components of planning might require implementing a process of achieving goals known as S.M.A.R.T. Goals. S.M.A.R.T stands for *specific, measurable, attainable, realistic,* and *timely.* These are a critical part of planning a business or working through any process, no matter the sector. Your brand is your business! As you plan various aspects of *your* business, you need to be S.M.A.R.T about it.

Another type or concept of branding is strictly centered on the organization of business ideas. That would include products, corporations, and other viable organizations like not-for-profits, whether ministry or social services organizations. Most times, profitable business or service organizations will let you know what makes them unique and how they are striving to be different and better than anyone else in their area of focus.

Corporate entities have more of a competitive edge versus that of the service industry. Apple versus Microsoft, Target versus Walmart, and McDonald's versus Burger King are same sector competitors that come to mind. Service groups do tend to focus on just that: serving. There usually are special demographics that help determine where their service is focused. If your customer base is in an urban community, the needs, requirements, and approach may differ greatly than that of an affluent suburban clientele. Overall, the same general approach for success might be applied to provide quality and to further the desire to make an impact. But the *way* you go about executing your plan will be the key determining factor. The approach to serve is likely as different as night and day with each client because of their designated area of focus and the situational dynamics.

A few years ago, a relocation project landed with a small community service organization where they needed to prepare groups of people living in a development to be moved into other areas of a major urban city. While several agencies had been given contracts, the one that was most successful in this process had employees who didn't necessarily have the higher level of degrees as those of other agencies.

The successful team managed to actually take the time to learn about the people in the area they serviced—their goals, their dreams, education level, or lack thereof. They focused on overcoming their fears and had the ability to deal with their anger about having their way of life changed so abruptly and against their will. Additionally, the team had to find ways of dealing with a criminal element of those who didn't respect the entire process in the least. So while degrees were well and fine on paper, the success rate was higher with those employees who had the heart to go in and put the focus on servicing the people, not on just collecting a paycheck.

Being a brand takes the view of your expertise to an entirely new level and perspective. It helps one to distinguish *how* what your organization has stands out from others in the same sector. Branding is working on you representing your brand (which is yourself) in the best possible light. Each one of those employees from that successful brand had one thing in common—achieving the end result in a manner that afforded the residents dignity, equity, and respect.

Ordered Steps

Do you have a clear direction of where you're going? Have you calculated what it's going to take for you to get there: required resources, potential profits, losses, etc.? Do you have a handle on the estimated time that is required to make your arrival to your desired goals?

There are a number of steps and an order for which we have to be diligent and clear when we set out to achieve a vision or a goal. The "vetting" of opportunities must become a pivotal part of our branding process. This is what I will easily refer to as "*the process of elimination*," also known as "*key prioritization*"; putting what's most pressing first!

Early in life, Woman A knows she desires the following things: college education, a career, a husband, and family. Woman B wants to travel the world and devote her life to a cause of social change. Each woman's set of desires are admirable, but completely different paths must be taken in order to reach the desired results. It will take a completely different set of priorities for Woman A to pursue her dreams than that of Woman B. Some of Woman A's desires are contingent on the outcome of another outside of her own self-control. She cannot marry herself, nor can she self-produce in the most traditional sense. Everything that Woman B wants to pursue is pretty much up to her immediate choices of timing and available resources.

As one holding the ultimate responsibility of how our brand is perceived, we must be strategic when identifying branding opportunities. No matter what our status is in life, we must take care when preserving our personal brand.

Celebrities are a great example to use in this case. Some actresses or actors, singers, and performers achieve a high level of success, then sometimes suddenly make one fatal mistake that changes everything. Some have allowed managers, mentors, family, or spouses to take them so far off their brand that they lose touch with reality; and with it, their audience and market who loved them for their *original* brand. With this change came a loss of opportunities in viable movie roles, or performance venues dried up, and with it, their finances.

In all reality, every idea presented to you may not be the best in the greater scheme of your scope of endeavors. When we originally decide that a plan is wonderful, this may not continue to be the case once the process of planning gets underway. I am specifically referring to creative ideas that you may want to implement and possible business opportunities that may also be presented to you. The "order" in which one approaches their projects, no matter how great or small, has to be strongly considered. Doing the *right thing* at the *wrong time* can be as equally detrimental as doing the *wrong thing* at the *wrong time*. In other words, being in sync with timing, opportunity, and preparedness in order to be successful will only come through proper planning and implementation.

Clearly, I am not implying that you should be so "rigid" or "cookie cutter" that you aren't willing to let the creative juices flow and maintain that inner *risk-taker mentality* in order to take on a certain level of risk. I encourage you to set out to do things in the order that will maximize the opportunities that have come your way. You can't prevent getting stuck in the sand sometimes, but by all means, having a plan means you won't stay there for long. Time management is essential. Be calculated and intentional on how you choose to divvy out your time in every area of your life.

Recently, two television shows seem to have captivated the American viewing audience in huge numbers. *Scandal* and *How to Get Away with Murder* are overtaking the ratings. On the largest social media venue two things happen during the time period that these shows are on: 1) postings of other things slow down; and 2) postings, memes, and exchanges about the shows reach an all-time high. One meme in particular points out how upset people are when anyone calls or comes to their home during this time. That's how important 60 minutes of entertainment has become—nothing else gets done except rear ends positioned in a comfortable chair and eyes glued to the screen taking it all in. Except commercial breaks. That's when people post their observations on social media or run to the fridge to get a snack.

Wouldn't it be wonderful if the approach to branding was even remotely similar? You designate a time to focus strictly on a particular area in your life and during that period, you don't allow distractions, interruptions, or hindrances—the focus is on that area. Every single day. Professional ice-skaters and gymnastic contenders set aside several hours to hone their skills. A published book doesn't materialize out of thin air. Writers who wish to become published authors set a deadline and write until they have a finished product, then engage the necessary people to take things a step further—editors, proofreaders, agents, etc. Singers would be highly embarrassed if they take the mic, the music cues up—and it's a song that they haven't taken the time to rehearse. Sound check is important, and many artists arrive hours before a concert is set to take place in order to make sure that everything is in place. The same holds true for you building your brand: planning, preparing, putting in work, engaging key people/mentors, and the execution of it all.

If you're considered a successful person at any stage of your life, then you are more than likely someone who does things differently than the average person. Why is that the case? Mostly because you're aware of at least some of the elements I've spoken of, but mainly, it's because you realize success and hard work go hand in hand. I believe those who have accomplished their goals and dreams have arrived to that desired plateau and have no doubt done so by being meticulous about what they've chosen to focus on in relation to their time and resources.

One of the best pieces of advice I've ever received in life has come from Mom. Her advice to her children has always been to focus on one thing at a time and do that one thing well. The heart of what she has attempted to have us consider is not to be a jack-of-all-trades, yet a master of none. From time to time, I've taken a moment to reflect on my work history. What I've come to realize is that there are points where I've become overextended in my focus when climbing the career or life ladder toward success.

Many times, people might know how life works in the literal sense of the word, but do not always have the luxury and ability to gear all of their efforts to focus in on just one thing. When that happens, many other tasks, goals, and dreams may go unattended or put on hold. For example, if you were working multiple jobs for a season in order to make ends meet, you will not have as much time to focus on other things because of your time being limited. There are only so many hours in a day. In addition to that, you are still responsible for your acts of daily living (grocery shopping, laundry, housework, paying your bills, and too many more to name). This scenario can play out in a number of different ways, but the key is not to lose sight of your goals, although you may not be able to focus on them temporarily.

But in the sense of planning and setting aspirations to reach significant landmarks, you must become keenly aware of how to focus, especially within the fast-paced world we live in today. Although you may not be able to do everything, you are able to do what you choose to do in an excellent way . . . where to place your time, focus, and energy to achieve a level of excellence that can clearly be identified as your brand.

Excellence Is a Key Ingredient . . .

How is excellence defined by you? Excellence has several meanings—it never settles; it is not the average. Excellence is a word that when applied, immediately places a demand and commitment that signifies *being above the rest*. The definition of excellence that I like the most is:

> *"The state of quality of excelling or being exceptionally good; extreme merit. An action, characteristic, feature, etc., in which a person excels."*
>
> (Cited from dictionary.reference.com)

So to walk in excellence, one must become *exceptional*. Having an expectation of "excellence" can provoke some level of fear in people who don't live by this standard. Being excellent requires one to strive to surpass just being *"typical* or *common."* That, in itself, for some individuals, can bring about a certain amount of pressure or anxiety. Have you ever been in a situation and observed someone getting upset just because the demand was put on them to improve their current status from satisfactory to a step above? Why someone would not want to be or do their very best is baffling, but many do settle for less than exceptional because they haven't been convinced that excellence is not an option but excellence is necessary.

My family can attest to how much I love to win. That competitive edge comes naturally since I am not the only in the family who has that trait. As a youth, I was fairly athletic, participating in high school sports, running indoor track for a year, and I played softball as well. I also participated in school government activities which stimulated the "intellectual" competitive side of me. At that stage of my life, anywhere "game-changer" opportunities were available, I wanted to be in the mix. Past high school, I continued to seek out or have been attracted to the type of opportunities that involve a challenge.

Competition has now taken on an entirely different path and meaning since it involves being more so in competition with "myself" as an adult. I've evolved to the point that I now have a new perspective on competition. Whether in character, health, education, or my own spiritual growth and development, my greatest purpose has been to become a better person. It's not just an outward focus, but it's been an inward one as well.

Some examples of personal development for me in times past has meant taking additional college courses beyond my degrees or seeking mentorship in a particular area that was directly related to a goal I had. Sometimes it simply has meant becoming more disciplined in my health and wellness to achieve a particular result. Being honest with myself has been the key to self-analysis (no matter how difficult) for the sake of improvement and holding myself accountable. Becoming your best self or brand means also being willing to address strengths as well as the shortcomings—equally. Continuing to live life in this manner will force you to practice what you preach. You will put yourself in check long before anyone else has a chance to.

While it might be reasonable to have expectations of others, you must first be willing to invoke those same high expectations onto yourself. Whether it's a professional, ministry, or service endeavor of any kind, try to encourage others to do their part by first attempting to do your best. There is no other way to move forward with high expectations of excellence from others subsequently if you aren't willing to be bent on executing those same expectations on yourself. Never expect from others what you're not willing to do yourself! This is the "precept by example" methodology.

There comes a point when excellence must shift from being a concept in the mind, to an action physically manifested. You can think about winning all day long, but if you haven't gotten off your butt to get in the game, it only remains a dream. You must be willing to do the work. When you do the work, others will then take notice and might want to emulate and follow suit of what you're doing.

Doing the work tends to open doors of opportunities. Sometimes unexpected ones may appear that you may not have even known existed before, simply because you are prepared and are in the right place at the right time. People who are willing to do the work many times further excel when seeing a model or blueprint because this shows them that it has been done and that it can be done.

The Excellence Approach

"The best of them are no more than you and the worse of them are no less than you."

—Bishop T. D. Jakes

The "excellence approach" is synonymous with "excellence in attitude." An attitude of excellence should always be a key ingredient of your branding formula. When one is working toward achieving a set goal, the intent must be striving for an outcome of being "your" very best. Excellence is about being above *your* norm; it's about *your* average. There are people who do "just enough" and people who go "above and beyond." You have to ask yourself which category you fall in. A simple example is . . .

Worker A walks through the office door every day at 9:07 a.m. (though starting time is 9:00 a.m.). She takes forever to get settled in, get her coffee, check personal social media and e-mails, and then her first words aren't "Good morning," they are, "Is it time to go yet?"

She just arrived—late—wasn't prepared to start on time, has a rag-gedy attitude toward work first thing, and will likely produce work and have an attitude and approach that reflects exactly that. Her inter-actions with her coworkers and the company are riddled with com-plaints, impatience, and grievances. This type of person is already defeated even before she arrives and definitely before she leaves (must I add 10 minutes before her end time, and that's also when she's already taken an extra 15 minutes coming back to the desk from lunch). Totally unbelievable, right? This is an example of a real true-life scenario, I might add.

Then take Worker B, who arrives about 15 minutes early, grabs coffee, organizes his desk, turns on the computer, and is raring to go at 9:00 a.m. This is the type of person who handles coworkers and clients alike with a professionalism that represents the company and himself, well. At 4:58, he looks at the clock and says, "Oh shoot. It's time to go. This day went by so fast!"

Two different people, one with a mediocre approach and the other with an eye for excellence. Which worker do you think will be in line for bonuses and promotions? Which worker do you think will be first in line for layoffs if the company goes into a massive overhaul?

Basically, it doesn't matter what you physically choose to do. You should strive toward being exceptional. If you're a teacher, then be the kind that is prepared for students, enthused about teaching, and excited about bringing the world of learning to the classroom. If you're a surgeon, be the type of surgeon that others in the field aspire to imitate. If you're a bus driver, be the type of driver who greets his or her passengers with a smile, and one who realizes that you are respon-sible for the lives of everyone on the bus.

Bishop Thomas Dexter (T. D.) Jakes, a best-selling author, world-renowned pastor, speaker, producer, husband, father, and friend to many around the globe, has often shared the story of how his father started a cleaning business years ago in their home state of West Virginia.

A Bucket and a Mop . . .

The bishop's father started a janitorial business with one bucket and one mop. According to Bishop Jakes, his father viewed his responsibility of mopping the same as creating a magnificent piece of art. His father's handling of a mop was as paint to a brush and the floor was his Picasso. Because this was the manner he saw fit to take care of his family, he treated his responsibility of mopping the floors as his "craft." There was so much care and pride taken in his effort of mopping a floor. His signature move was to "pop the mop" whenever he completed the job to his own satisfaction. As a result of his work and commitment to the idea of excellence, he was able to create a cleaning business and staffed a number of workers, who believed and took on his same work ethic. How magnificent is that?

Often, I take the time to reflect on this story when I think of the process and steps to being excellent, particularly from the vantage point of working only with the resources you've been given access to and having the mind-set to only settle for being the best. Because he chose to work in an excellent way (with his bucket and a mop), he exploded with so much more than he probably could have ever imagined. He became a profitable business owner, leading over 40 employees (if I recall the number correctly) at a time and in a place where this was certainly quite uncommon, mostly due to the culture of the day in this region and at that time.

This story has been repeated in Bishop Jakes's sermons as a framework for his own self-described meager beginnings and his now great ascension to many levels of success in both ministry and in business. My understanding is his father's cleaning business was quite successful in its own right, which was primarily based on his way of choosing to approach the work he was doing. As a result, he went on to grow the business, first leading by example. What I gather the most from this particular story is that one must have a passion in and for excellence, even in something that might seem minor to everyone else.

Truly, this lesson surpasses the "just mopping floors," but more along the lines of not merely *what* you do, but *how* you do it. I will say that there is an army of everyday people all over the world who still take much pride in their work (what they produce) in the midst of societies that have a deteriorating mind-set and no concept of what good work ethics and customer service looks like. The key component to carrying out a task in excellence is the way you actually think before you ever start.

A local elementary school crossing guard is stationed right in the community where I live. Of course, I've seen many crossing guards in my life, but there is something completely special, by far, in the way this particular one does her job. First, it is quite visible that she clearly takes pride in the work that she does. The care and the way that she wears her uniform is clearly evident in the fact that she's crisply suited and booted from head to toe, literally. The way in which she carries her sign and her stance proudly proclaims, "I am someone of importance, and I have a job to do!" I don't know exactly what she's doing differently than all the other crossing guards in the world, but she gives what I would best describe as a sense of "pageantry" to her assignment, waving to each and every passerby, if but for only a split second with a greeting. Even with my car windows normally being up when I pass her post, I don't hear her, but I do see her mouth move and her smile as she is voicing her greeting gracefully. She also makes eye contact or sometimes offers a simple nod with a great big ole smile accompanying that wave. I don't know the formula of how she does it, but all I can say is, she, indeed, does it well. I also make sure that I speak and wave back to her after she shares her "good morning." She obviously loves what she's doing and her sense of excellence and passion are easily identifiable. They stick out like a neon light in the dark.

Everyone has been endowed with special gifts and talents. Part of your journey is self-discovery. Life must become a complete perspective of how you fit in it if you expect to fulfill your purpose by utilizing all of your gifts and talents. Never minimize or "dumb down" your gifts or talents because of others' discomfort. Keep on shining so that your light will impact others in a way that you could have never imagined.

Start Small but Think Big!

One role that has always fascinated me has been that of a lead singer in a band or music group. I've wondered what that feeling could be like to prepare for a sold-out concert or appear on a venue's big stage. Imagine a stadium filled with thousands upon thousands of adoring fans and being given the opportunity to perform for them. I'm certain that for any music artist this would be the epitome of a dream that has come true—*the ultimate arrival.* To live out your purpose and act on your passions in this way would be simply indescribable.

When I was a child, I would pretend to be a music superstar like many other children. I created a makeshift microphone, got into wardrobe, hit the "play" button, and practiced a song over and over in my bedroom until I got everything down pat. Of course, it was completely necessary to have a mirror nearby just so that I could have the ability to capture these moments while acting out my role. I needed to "see" myself in action. I did my own dress rehearsals, sound checks, and main performances while pretending to be this "superstar" singer. Oh, the places a child's imagination can take them. So many components must go into accomplishing your dreams. Imagery, "life" rehearsals, a great deal of the investment of time, money, resources, and, of course, an undying faith and sure belief that it can be achieved.

Staying with the example of a music artist, there must be a fully orchestrated strategic marketing plan in order for the artist to be successful. The media campaign alone must be well thought out and includes: social media, television, online, print, and radio campaigns, just to name a few. Talent plays an integral part, but it's not the only ingredient to an artist's success. The artist also must be willing and able to tour and make live appearances to share their talents with the world. To make it to the top and stay there doesn't "happen" merely by chance or simply by being liked by the masses. A total *packaging*, or as it's often referred to nowadays—"bundling" must occur in order for an artist of any kind to become a national or global phenomenon.

Building a strong brand is quite similar. It's about being effectively marketed to and for the masses. People will "buy-in" if they "believe-in" you. There is indeed a certain amount or level of raw talent that an artist must possess. Don't get me wrong; although talent can take you far, talent alone is never enough. Although I will expound on the other critical topics concerning branding in this chapter, part of it evolves around character, attitude, integrity, and other factors.

One major brand artist comes to mind who definitely embodies the epitome of a multifaceted entertainment brand—Beyoncé. Love it, hate it, take it, or leave it, the power behind her personal brand has always been a force to be reckoned with. Very few people on the planet have not been exposed to her work in some way. Despite what anyone thinks about her as a singer, dancer, or actress, the one thing everyone can give her credit for is being a shrewd businesswoman with the kind of team backing her that many would "live" for. In addition to major music successes with sales of millions upon millions of records, she also has major endorsement deals in the areas of cosmetics, perfume, and the soda industry. She's also a Grammy Award–winning songwriter and has backed a fashion empire in honor of her late grandmother known as the House of Dereon, which sells everything from jeans to shoes. From her music to acting, from business dealings and philanthropy, all of these activities, combined, have all played a significant role in the creation of her personal brand empire.

A major factor that is so important to her story is the commitment by her parents and family at such an early age. Their support for her ambition and that of the original girl group in her formative years catapulted her into the realm of up-and-coming artists. In other words, she was not an "overnight" success. A great deal of blood, sweat, and tears were likely shed along the way.

Beyoncé is also known for her killer work ethic as it's been said many times over by her industry colleagues in various media outlets. So let's ponder on the topic of *work ethic* for a moment. What is it really? A belief that the way you approach what you do brings a moral satisfaction; therefore, great care and concentration is put into it. Hard work plays a major role in the success of any budding or established artist. There will always be someone who is a little more talented, gifted, qualified, or seemingly more "ideal." But no one should ever work more or harder than you when it comes to your brand. Nothing will ever replace good old-fashioned hard work, which is identified as your level of commitment to your purpose. Everything you execute in your life should be done in a strategic manner. Begin to be intentional and clear about your goals. When you put in the time and energy, you will make progress toward meeting them.

There's a slogan in some religious circles that been repeated over the years:

"If you make one step, God will make two."

In other words, when you actually start making moves toward the things you are destined to do, inexplicable things happen that combine with faith to believe that will get you there. With this kind of faith and undying belief . . . nothing shall be impossible.

3

WHAT'S IN A NAME? EVERYTHING!

Brand is all about Presentation, Presentation, Presentation!

W*hat's in a name?"* One of the greatest questions posed from one of the world's most famous writers—William Shakespeare. And, yes, I was born and raised a Shakespeare in case this question had crossed your mind. Though, in another vein, I've always found the study of Shakespeare to be quite fascinating. Especially his poetic tragedy of star-crossed lovers, *Romeo and Juliet*, where one of his most famous questions is posed: *"What's in a name?"* I'm certain some of you may have asked where he, Shakespeare, was going with this statement. Or was it actually "she," since this is the famous line written for Juliet, one of the main characters from the story.

The history behind this famous line in its context would be the scene where Juliet is letting Romeo know that although their families are practically at war with one another, she will not let this deter her from her love for him. Romeo is so moved with passion by her love toward him that he denounces his family's name. In those times, there was so much value tied to lineage, which, of course, included the surname. So in my context of posing this famous line, *"What's in a name?"* my answer would have to be: *everything!*

Your name is key; it represents you. It's the central point of reference of who you are or what you represent as a person, product, or organization. When someone speaks a name, it is automatically associating them with something. Whether quality, integrity, or the lack thereof, a name can speak volumes in more ways than one. When I hear *Steve Jobs*, I automatically think *Apple*; when I hear *Macy's*, I think *retail giant*. So as I think of Apple, I think technology takeover based on what I've heard, especially in recent business reports of Apple's earning position, which is well on its way to earning a trillion dollar in sales. When I think of Macy's, I think of a retail fixture, a company that has endured the test of time and is still thriving.

Your name also represents your reputation. Your name, and more importantly, what you do with your name, will become a mirror of your reputation as well. This is one of the most important pieces of your brand that you must guard with diligence. *"What's in a name?"* In many cultures, a child is given the first name of one grandparent, and the middle name of another in order to bestow a simple slice of lineage upon the newborn. In some families, the first girl child is named after a beloved aunt or maybe even one who is deceased—all in efforts to maintain a sense of continuity in a family line. In many circles, people are encouraged to be careful what name they place on a child because early on, it becomes a sort of brand.

"What's in a name?" This one line, which has gone down in theatrical history, identifies the central struggle of Shakespeare's play. In our society, there was a time in history when people guarded their family name and reputations as if their very lives depended on it. This was so because their lives were tied to what their name represented. One

manner in which their reputation was guarded is the way that business affairs were handled. I distinctly think of my father who was cut from the cloth of men who vigorously guarded their personal affairs, in particular, his credit. He took so much pride in being a man, handling his financial affairs with diligence, and maintaining an A+ credit rating. No one, I repeat—no one—would be allowed to interfere with how he maintained his business affairs. We have to be equally deliberate as we guard our brand's name.

Brand Mix

There are key ingredients that go into branding yourself successfully; what I would call "brand nonnegotiables." So many things dominate our time nowadays; school, work, special projects, you name it. Everyone seems to be superbusy, and no one wants to feel like they are wasting time. "None," to be precise, can afford to be wasted. People with purpose and who are intentional about their lives tend to also be the same about their time. Making the best, most-lasting, and positive impressionable brand means coming out the gate with those elements being your original intent. Live passionately and purposely.

Regardless of your walk in life, where you're from, "literally," *or* the *point* you are in your life; no matter where from a socioeconomically perspective, age, stage, or gender . . . This statement holds true: *You* are *your* brand! What people see is what people believe they will truly get. That's why the emphasis cannot be made enough on how much you should take care of your personal presentation. You are representing you at all times, and *no one* can represent you better than you. Showing up for life is just like going for a job interview. If you want to be considered a viable candidate for a job, you must prepare yourself for the interview. No matter what industry, the question you must always ask is: *What is going to make me stand out above all the rest? What can I bring to the table that supersedes the other candidates?*

Let's be honest, there are so many people who are looking for jobs that employers can now take their time to pick the individual that they really want. In such a competitive market, having the qualifications is a start, but arriving with the proper attire and being able to articulate why you're the best candidate for the position is also a must. Expect to participate in an in-depth questioning session about your background and personal experiences and to share how you meet the qualifications for the position. Before gracing their doorstep, at least take the time to do some research on the organization to ensure it is a place you'd like to hang your hat. This is not intended to be an interview advice book, per se, but it's all interconnected with the idea of you being a brand.

Recently, I walked into a local retail store and made a beeline to the jewelry section. As I made it to the counter, I waited for the salesclerk to wrap up her transaction with the current customer. The customer drew my attention. My impression was that she had to be some sort of business executive based on her accessories, the tailored suit, and her stance. She was indeed well polished and appeared to be very organized.

When the clerk stepped away to check the price of an item, the customer spoke to me, and I responded and also noted the store's wonderful deals and sales. After a bit of small talk, I asked where she worked, only to learn that she was retired. Not only was she retired, but she had worked on the police force. Based on how she chose to represent herself, I would never have thought her to be from the law enforcement profession. She seemed too nice; her demeanor was pleasant and warm. Sad to say, those traits are not the first, or even second, image that comes to my mind when thinking of police officers on a typical day.

She then began to talk about how much she loved dressing up, and especially now that she was free to do so as a retiree. She conveyed her elation about being able to wear her own things instead of a police uniform. I thought she was definitely in a leadership role (i.e., president, vice president) in a field of a business nature.

The point I want to make is that her appearance and the way she carried herself made me categorize her in the way that I did. I was interpreting the present and formulated a story of who she was in my mind. Her actual reality never factored into it. Overall, she represented her brand, which was *herself*. The bottom line is there must be great care taken in being the best of who we are.

You should always strive to position yourself to wear fashion that complements who you are. This is extremely important and in most instances, it reflects how you will be viewed on all other levels of your presentation. These are indicators of how you're willing to represent yourself and willing to present your brand to others. Research says anything done consistently for 21 days straight becomes a habit. As humans, we are forever a work in progress, something I would label as "projects of improvement." For example, the simple action of running a Saturday morning errand, and the manner in which it's done, can drastically impact our brand and its perception

Although exchanges like this can be short, they can draw on a number of factors. I know it may seem a little uncomfortable for some to begin to think from such a "me-centered" angle, but for the purposes of driving this point home, I need to point out these few factors. It's vital that there is a clear picture in your mind about how representing you deeply affects your relationships and opportunities to connect with people, but most of all, yourself. I believe that everyone is important and that all life must be respected. But more importantly, most individuals must begin to understand their own *personal importance*. Having an "inner clarity" that you are unique and special is important as it signifies your ability to connect to your purpose in life. The very first thing that anyone sees about you is you.

Take readers, for instance. It's always been said that you shouldn't judge a book by its cover. Truthfully, that's the first thing that readers will see when considering the purchase of a book. Then they'll flip over to the back cover and read the text, followed by cracking open that first page to read that opening line, the next paragraph, the next page, and so on. If a reader is turned off by the cover, it's less likely they'll go through the rest of the process to find out what the book is about or if it's worth buying. Your physical appearance (the visual you) will always be the first thing that represents who you are. Then your presence (the aura, persona, and personality) that you carry is equally noted.

Sometimes, certain people can come into your presence, and you'll have an instant connection with them. They are warm, they are inviting. And, sometimes, I've come into the presence of individuals and feel an instant cold aura, almost like a breeze because they were very impersonal which left me with a bad feeling. There is a quote that I love by the late Maya Angelou who said: *"I've learned that people will forget what you said, people will forget what you did, but people will never forget how you made them feel."* These are such powerful words from such a prolific woman who had experienced so much in her lifetime. Maya did so many things in her life and was "hailed as one of the great voices of contemporary black literature" and as a Renaissance woman. Her work in *I Know Why the Caged Bird Sings* is a chronicle of her life up to the age of 16, and it received critical and commercial success as she recounts a "self-awakening" of the younger Angelou. She endured many hardships and reinventions of her life, proving that one's brand is, indeed, constantly evolving.

I truly believe there are some things that only you can do on this earth in the uniqueness of who you are and what you were created to be. *So how does this apply to being branded or a brand?* When I researched the definition for the word *branded*, I found two one-word definitions given: *labeled* or *categorized*. When I reviewed the definitions for *brand*, I found a number of different definitions, of course, but I think the one I will share is the closest to identify based on the topics covered in this book:

> A brand is a unique design, sign, symbol, words, or a combination of these, employed in creating an image that identifies a product and differentiates it from its competitors. Over time, this image becomes associated with a level of credibility, quality, and satisfaction in the mind. Thus, brands help harried consumers in the crowded and complex marketplace, by standing for certain benefits and value. (Reference:Error! Hyperlink reference not valid.)

Overall, you have to realize that you have a voice and something great to contribute to the world because you are here. Only then can you proceed to make the impact you were intended to make.

Brand Influencers

Many of us are groomed in the early stages or the formative years of life to become the persons we are to be. Based on the stage, the age, and experiences one may have garnered in life, the goals, interests, and finding ultimate purpose will be drastically different from person to person. You will not, in most cases, be the first and only one to do what you do as a chosen career or vocation. The good news is, however, no one will ever be able to do it quite like you. No one will encounter or touch people in your circle of the world exactly the way you will.

For example, there are many who choose to become an athlete, a doctor, a politician, or a musician. However, there is a greater reality . . . everyone will not become a *professional* athlete, a world-renowned surgeon, or be inducted into the Hollywood Walk of Fame. And that's okay too, because even those who don't achieve that level still can have an established pattern of excellence in order to determine what their own level of success is in their sphere of the globe. Establishing a "personal best" set of goals and making every attempt to achieve them will help you understand your significance and value. The world functions and revolves around people with similar and variant paths, who may fall into similar patterns of thinking, but none of them own a DNA and life that is exactly alike.

Then we have a group I will term as the *direct, indirect influencers*. The media is a great example of a direct, indirect influencer. This sole group of individuals creates campaigns for, targets, interacts with, and helps you form opinions about people, topics, and behaviors, and you've never necessarily met these reporters. Of course, there are different types of media influences. The news *should be* reporting the facts. In most instances, they rely heavily on their reports without sometimes knowing for sure that they have the full story. Society has been generally programmed to believe what they see and hear in the media. I can't tell you how many times, especially recently, where false reporting frequently takes place.

Another great influence is our spiritual belief system. Our beliefs tend to overshadow and affect much of what we do with our lives, especially as adults. This proves how much we are really active in our faith, which are the principals we live by. These principals can determine who we choose to marry, and it can form our outlook on the shaping of the execution of ethics and moral character. Our behavior in various situations is also determined based on our beliefs. It can be the restraint of our behaviors in certain situations or even possibly the lack thereof. You may have been brought up to believe an eye for an eye and a tooth for a tooth. Someone else may believe in turning the other cheek, which are both indeed very different concepts.

If everyone had the capacity to be the same, universities would not implement acceptance requirements and a standardized number of expectations. First, the application process matches that have the mental acuity that matches with the school's standards, guidelines, and expectations. Second, they ask for essays on particular subjects so that they're able to gauge whether you can formulate a coherent series of thoughts. Next, comes the personal interview to learn more about your "brand" in person and whether you're a good fit for the program for which you've applied. No, they're not looking for cookie-cutter students, but they are wanting to ensure that your goals and what they have to offer in the form of education will align. They're preparing you to be able to compete on a global level, and perhaps catapult further an idea or process that's already in existence.

You can still make your individual mark, even though you are not the first to do a particular thing. The onus is on you to bring your unique style or signature mark, and that is what will make the difference and cause your individual brand to be something of value. When choosing when and how to capitalize on opportunities that exhibit great potential in furthering your personal brand, you should consider certain things.

If there is a situation that needs to be let go, like a bad relationship after a good length of time and then, staying in it with the hopes that things will simply get better may not be the best approach. You may have to let go of the relationship and everything associated with it.

It is important to identify those who can add to your knowledge levels in the areas where you may fall short. Everyone has a certain amount of experiences in various areas; however, others have more. Branding yourself is indeed a journey that you should not go on alone. These relationships must be nurtured in a way that embodies both trust and understanding in order to become effective.

4

AUTHENTICITY: BE AUTHENTIC, BE YOU

No one develops into a wonder overnight, and that also holds true for your brand. You have to willing to make the necessary sacrifices to commit to achieving any goal or dream. There is no way around hard work and being dedicated. There is a process to life, and it begins even before we're born.

First and foremost, the seed is planted into a mother's womb. After a time of incubation and ultimately delivery, the baby is born. When a baby enters this world, it is completely dependent on caregivers. The baby is fed, nurtured, and goes from an infant to a toddler, at which stage many of the fine motor skills are honed. Then, eventually, the focus turns toward gross motor development. There is no such thing as "overnight" in human development. As one grows and plateaus, there is now a commitment to lifetime development, which also involves various components of intellectual achievement.

The direction you choose to take after maturing to adulthood is completely up to you; even though you might run into an obstacle or circumstance that is completely out of your control. For example, maybe you had plans and goals to finish college, get married, start a family, buy a house in the suburbs, make six figures, travel the world by 40, and retire before the legal retirement age. You've probably had some type of discussions with other individuals, or maybe even yourself, in this regard. Unfortunately, things don't always play out exactly as planned, and that means being flexible and figuring out solutions on the spot. When you choose to stay on course, even if there's a slight detour in working toward your dream's original goals, you'll arrive to many of your "destinations" in time, and sometimes sooner than ever expected. You have to trust that when you do the work, that the right plan is unfolding for your life.

A mixture of time, life experiences, and circumstances all formulate our life's path. There is no magic potion to conquer this thing called life.

I was pondering recently on the amazing process of the basic science of how we enter the world as human beings and end up in our various families. Skipping the lesson on the birds and the bees, however, I want you to think about the wider context of how two unique individuals come together and create a life. Now you exist, and your path in this world as it relates to who you're forever connected to is set.

All of us have our own unique identities that tend to replicate characteristics or traits of our parents. Your life is an initial reflection of how the culture of what you call "home" and call "family" is established. No one could have asked for a different ride into this world even if they wanted to; however, making a story with a desired outcome is the determination of the direct choices that are made on a day-by-day basis. The knowledge and cultivation instilled within us in the formative years has a deep impact on the foundation for our personal development. What you believe, based on the influence of parents, siblings, other relatives, friends, acquaintances, other critical friends, and the influence of society as a whole, aids in the makeup of the unique individual you have become. But who we choose to become as we mature has as much to do with the very core of the actions taken.

Clearly, what is passed along to you in developmental seasons in your life's journey will affect your brand tremendously. You must be willing to take an ongoing and hard first look at who you are, then determine if you're on the path of becoming who you want to be. Whether you're a person coming into your own as a youth, young adult, or a mature adult, you must continue to take a personal inventory of your life, appraisals, or "brand shapers," and acknowledge the areas that need to be addressed. And if that means drawing on the present before you get to your future as a means to achieve that end, do so. Build from right where you are!

Think about your influencers. Oftentimes, we read about them, follow their lives, and admire them all from a distance. You might not ever actually meet them personally, but they impact you just by being who they are. In a real sense, we've been impacted by their brand, the essence of who they are. They've put in the work, and their brand is highly inspirational and is something you can draw on. This very fact should lead to self-evaluation. It must become a part of the growth steps regardless of an individual's status. Knowing who you are and how you want to proceed with your brand is a critical component to moving forward in branding and in life.

Seize the Moment

Sometimes people are considered an *overnight success story*, but there is no such thing in the true sense of the word. You have limited knowledge about what steps it has taken to prepare them for this point in their lives. What is it that makes someone go from being recognized on a local or regional level to a national or a global level? If life's formula was that easy to figure out, everyone would be a taker. A number of circumstances have transpired to catapult someone into transcending into the person they were destined to become. They seized on an opportunity and momentum to the point that they became . . . a brand.

Don't Miss Your Moment: The Art of Momentum

No matter what, I knew I had to prepare for the next thing I wanted to do because certain opportunities will only present themselves at certain times. At some point after creating goals, it becomes a "now" time to take the necessary actions to achieve them. There is indeed a time and season for everything to occur in the world. When it comes down to branding, only you will know your "season." A season, as generally known, is characterized as times during the year when particular weather conditions affect temperatures and atmospheric experiences. In the basic sense, there are typically four seasons: spring, summer, fall, and winter. Depending on the part of the country in which you reside, you can experience all of them or at least some of them. One thing that proves to be true is that each season leads to totally different states of living and states of mind. In winter, I feel more like a warrior. The enemy, for me, is the snow and the cold in the Midwest. I feel as if I'm always fighting to conquer the intense conditions the winter weather brings. Now, in the spring, my frame of mind is all about considering "new beginnings." It's about having newness and starting over. Summertime, for me, tends to be a time to reflect, get out into the elements, and just enjoy some fun in the sun. The fall I use as an additional time of reflection, leading to the idea of harvest, seeing my results. I ask myself, have I made significant strides toward my goals? What have I accomplished? This is the time that I should be able to see and pinpoint what I have been working toward. And just as there's a need to decipher what to do in natural seasons, it's imperative and a must to know how to approach the seasons of personal branding in our lives. You must ask yourself, am I in a preparation period? Is it time to be aggressive in order to move forward? Or should I stand still?

Several things might cause someone to miss an opportunity, but the greatest of them all, in my opinion, is being ill prepared. How can you seize something you aren't ready to handle? Like a teenager having such a great desire to get a driver's license . . . without ever taking the time for driving lessons or studying for the test. You must prepare yourself for where you're going and make sure special attention is paid to the time which you've designated to accomplish everything.

Taking ownership of your own time and deadlines can be the hardest thing. I've always aspired to be on the fast track when it comes to my career goals, though it doesn't mean those opportunities happen as fast as I would like, and that track might swerve and bend along the way.

When you think of any organization, there are only so many positions available at any given time. If the turnover in the place you're working or in your chosen field is low, it will be much more difficult to make those jobs move because of positions remaining occupied. Sometimes, it's necessary to open your options to new places and opportunities. With that in mind, when the ideal opportunities present themselves where you are, the question then becomes, am I prepared? If the answer is no, then that might prevent a likely consideration for a promotion. Who knows when certain opportunities will come around again? On the other hand, if your answer is yes, let the competing begin!

As I reflect on moving from business to education, it was indeed an interesting experience that required a conscious decision and much soul-searching. Months before, I engaged in a great deal of research so I would make an easier transition. Because I had prepared myself, it seems as though the opportunities presented themselves. During that time, an accelerated pilot program for professionals entering the field of education came through. When opportunity meets preparation, it can truly work in your favor. You have no idea when something will be presented to you, but none of it will matter if you aren't prepared.

The Whole in Holistic. Attract What You Want

When the choice is made to become consistent in every area of our life, this requires a great amount of discipline. But then and only then should you expect to see better results. One must begin to understand that all areas of our lives are interlocked; all things affect the other. Your health affects your wealth, and your wealth affects your quality of life, and so on. All affecting factors are a result of choices made on a daily basis. It's like saying you want to be a wellness coach, and yet, you don't possess the ambition to set standards high enough to embody the very thing you're teaching others to become. You can't coach as effectively about something you have not experienced yourself.

I've always been driven in most areas of my life, but a little more in others. Being a high achiever in academics and my career have always been important to me. I've constantly sought out opportunities and responsibilities to prepare myself for the promotion that hadn't yet materialized. And that also included taking inventory of other areas of my life that could use some improvement. People are motivated as far as their careers (money) and their home life (earthly endeavors) but are not so willing to put the same tenacity into their spiritual well-being or health and wellness. Those too are part of your brand.

Evaluate Yourself

One must have the ability to *self-evaluate* in truth and honesty as it is a great part of defining the elements of our personal brand. See everything for what it is. Seek to bring clarity to the goals you've set for yourselves by clearly determining the steps to take in order to accomplish them. In this way, you become aware of the season you're in, can make the necessary corrections needed, and are less likely to become "stagnate."

The phrase "seize the moment" brings to mind a flash, something quick and fleeting. Many people make the attempt to customize their individual path and pace, and it might not be at the same pace as everyone else's. I should never be expected to run your race, nor am I expected to run at the same pace as you, and neither should you compare your pace or race to mine. That's how people get "stuck" believing that they're not doing as well as the next person.

The ultimate idea, however, is having a way to measure whether you're constantly in motion at your pace to achieve. Keeping it going, or as the term nowadays goes, "keep it moving," is the key to maximizing your potential that will lead to maximizing your purpose in life. This can also be a point of discovery . . . the moment when one recognizes the "something" in our life that needs to drastically change is in us, to create something better. So whether a moment of self-discovery now propels you to dismiss the old in order to welcome the new, these moments are quite critical to the well-being of your future success.

5

BRANDING LEVELS

Often, the beginning investment resources going into brand development must come from your own pocket. Your brand level is the onset of the way you are perceived by the world, and regardless of where you begin, this is the beginning of how to effectively promote your talent.

When considering the structure of the music industry, A&R representatives work on the careers of both new and existing recording artists. One of their main responsibilities is to showcase their client's talent in relation to others on the same trajectory and in the overall industry itself. A record label wants *all* of their artists to sell units, but how they position the artist to do this is the "brainchild." Once the contract is signed, a massive undertaking of investment goes into establishing the artist. All of a sudden, a particular artist will "burst on the scene" as the public begins to witness the massive amounts of marketing put into that artist. Often these massive efforts become responsible for catapulting an artist who is virtually unknown into newer heights of stardom. In the past, producing and presenting vast volumes of artists to the masses was referred to as putting them into "marketing machines." The optimum goal was public esteem and success for the artist, substantial earnings for the record label, and an established following that meant residual cash flowing in everyone's bank accounts. One opportunity combined with fame landed an artist exactly where he desired to be.

What's Good for the Goose . . .

Though the major campaign model has worked for some, keep in mind that every opportunity is not necessarily good, and even the good ones won't guarantee one to become an "overnight success." But it is important to recognize which is which. Investing only in what matters *the most* as it relates to our projects and our brand must not be riddled with compromise. Optimizing what's important means we are also considering what will bring our greatest return. Notice that I'm not implying that some potential projects don't matter or aren't good, but the ability to understand the timing and value of a said project is critical.

Following are some basic principles that will yield results:

1. Have clear vision

2. Follow through on your plan

3. Anticipate the potential obstacles

4. Stay focused through completion

Have Clear Vision

When I think of clarity in vision, the thought of possible distractions is always there. We should strive to "see clearly" when the rain of life comes down and all other obstacles appear. The rain can be a symbolism for many things that we can potentially face in our lives, which includes circumstances, fears, you name it, and the list goes on. Clear vision is a must to pave a clear road or path. I may be able to see all obstacles in my way . . . but I'm going move them out of the way.

That's why so many people have vision boards. This definitely solidifies the *where you want to go* piece. The hard work is the *how* in getting there. The hard work represents all the necessary measures you will need to "do" to bring your vision to life.

The approach to our brand and our business makes me think of how many times one can tend to focus on things that aren't important, when you should have your attention on what is critical. That's what a vision board does—keeps you focused on what you want. Sometimes the obstacles are ones we don't want to acknowledge actually as obstacles. Family, friends, coworkers, spouses, people who could be more supportive . . . but find ways to not be instead.

Imagine being in a forest or a jungle covered in a thick layer of fog and not being able to see for miles around. The trees and foliage tower over you in the never-ending reach for the sky. Then picture the uneven surfaces you'll have to cross. With this view, it would be impossible to navigate safely. If you are able to move, it's at a much-slower pace because you're unsure what you may encounter along the way. Besides the obvious terrain, wild animals and insects (which symbolize everyday distractions in this scenario) would also have you on high alert. Some level of attention would be focused on them instead of putting all efforts in getting through the jungle and to your destination. So, you're navigating shaky terrain, keeping an eye out on your surroundings, and still trying to get there. I would define this situation as a *triple distraction*. Isn't that how life really works?

Most everyone will admit to encountering stumbling blocks in life, like people who are distractors. Then we also endure interferences by time snatchers, like social media and television. I consider myself to be tech and media savvy, but I still have to consider the way each could potentially devour my time. My day starts early and ends late, so I do have to limit the amount of time I spend using social media. It's so addictive! If I don't time myself, and I do surpass it sometimes, I end up "surfing," get involved with the latest dialogue, wishing family and friends happy birthday . . . You name it! It's so easy to get sucked into social media sites. I would get much less done if I don't set boundaries on its daily use.

Everyone has different obstacles in this course called life. There are so many other things that could also be mentioned here, and if you're not careful, any of them could throw you completely off your path. We cannot allow unclear vision, broken focus, or obstacles to overpower us when it comes to our brand.

You can't let the opinions of others hold you back. In most cases, haters are those who may know of you but do not really have an interest in your success based on negative characteristics like jealousy, envy, coveting, etc. As one of my friends said, and I quote, "Don't worry about what 'they' say. T.H.E.Y. = The Haters Envying You. Remember that when you deal with haters, it's mind over matter. Pay them no mind because (what) they (think) don't really matter."

Show Resilience: "Saying" and "Doing" Are Two Totally Different Endeavors . . .

The business side of me is always thinking "holistically" regarding my projects and where I should devote my attention. The critical role is that moving forward toward those goals in the sequence chosen to accomplish them impacts how the future is played out. Wasting time and effort on unfruitful endeavors is not beneficial in any way. In order to "achieve" what you have set out to do, it requires a certain amount of resilience. It also requires the right order and timing.

Although this may sound very simplistic, ask yourself, am I a finisher or a procrastinator? Are you willing to accept the truth of what the answer is? Are you willing to tell yourself the truth? One of the hardest things for most people to address sometimes is the truth about themselves. Take inventory of the projects or endeavors you've been involved in over the years. Then tally up the level of attention given to them to bring them to completion. Don't worry, you're in good company. You'd likely be quite astonished by the number of folks who never complete things. That might have been your old reality/brand, but identifying it now gives you the opportunity to break that pattern and set new standards.

When I first had thoughts about college before actually going there, I was that student who felt that I had to make a hard line career decision that would be the main part of my life for a long, long time. I learned through life and experiences that an easy path simply would not be the case.

Resilience is a mind-set or inner ability to rebound no matter what life's obstacles are thrown at you. Think of horror flicks like the *Friday the 13th* franchise. To date, there were 12 films made over a 10-year period. How many times did Jason just keep coming back? Every time. And that is how *you* must be. No matter what comes or goes, you have to become known as the person who keeps coming back. A resilient person will never give up.

How many times have prominent historical figures shown us the art of not giving up and who went on to establish an undeniable imprint in earth's humanity quilt? From politicians to presidents, from athletes to artists, there is a certain fiber of relentlessness that is dominant in those who possess resilience. Think of all the times when all odds were against you, the mountain was insurmountable, and you couldn't see your way. Did you fold? Did you break? Or did you come out swinging?

Resilience. You do have it in you.

Don't Become Paralyzed

On the opposite extreme of resilience resides a debilitating condition known as "paralysis analysis." This condition manifests in the form of fear; when one tends to overthink every step they take to the extent that they fail to do anything. Think of being baptized in cement. This condition is equivalent to that.

Fear should be used as a springboard to *propel* one to a destination that's been never seen, although where we're headed may be considered "the unknown." Take joy in being allowed new experiences. Overcoming fear has a ton to do with perspective.

Most people become paralyzed simply because they are afraid of all of the unknown factors. Don't get me wrong; it takes a strong sense of trust to step out and do things that you are not comfortable doing. Most people love to stay in their comfort zone and never be challenged.

Everyone feels a certain amount of fear or anxiety when tackling something new. But don't let that stop you. View new experiences as opportunities to expand and express. We should work toward the expansion or growth of our platform in order for our reach to become bigger. The level and access to media is definitely the way communication has been accepted by people to reach the masses in society today.

6

LIVING OUT
YOUR TRUTH

This chapter addresses some personal truths that so many tend to gloss over. Behavior plays a heavy role in brand imaging. Behaviors, to a great extent, represent who we are at the core. We must take responsibility for decisions we make in relation to what we're trying to achieve. For example, you're taking the time to sow good seeds to reap excellent benefits . . . combined with action. Action and accountability . . . This all lays a good foundation to live in truth. Part of that is recognizing that integrity, honesty, and responsibility should take a front seat.

Many have fallen into a particular behavior that has become epidemic. And since I'm venturing into a personal playground that might be "delicate," I'm going to drop this little nugget right here . . .

One should not stand in "faith" believing that another person's husband or wife is theirs. There. I said it. And if this hits a nerve, it should. How often have we heard of people's lives, families, and careers destroyed, all because integrity took a backseat to indiscretions?

Clearly, if a man and a woman are already legally married, they have made a commitment and a covenant. Marriage is a legally binding agreement. So, to anticipate that you will have a relationship with a person that is already married on the basis that they are going to be yours one day is simply ludicrous. By the life standards of some, this is considered immoral behavior.

I've never seen a time like I do in today's society where so many people are willing to compromise in almost any type of situation in order to get what they want . . . whether students and grades or adults trying to climb the ladder of success. I've seen people be willing to do "anything" to ensure they receive a benefit that wasn't necessarily theirs to have. Turn on any local or national news show, or what I enjoy, crime scene investigation shows (which are typically the extreme examples) and this behavior seems to occur frequently, not only in our country, but in many other parts of the world.

My parents came from the generation of "your word is your bond," and that is the way I was brought up. My dad always told me, "Your word is everything. Once people can't depend on your word, that's everything." I know you might say, who listens to their parents nowadays? Well, I learned early on that doing things my way versus what my parents were telling me wouldn't work out. I simply wasn't that kid that wanted to just keep beating my head up against the wall.

Another example causing some discomfort to hear about is financial accountability. Your relationship with money is just as important as any other relationship. For example, it's not okay to write bad checks for money that does not exist in your bank account. And to that end, to avoid reconciling the debt and/or situation with the involved parties can leave a bad taste in one's mouth. Paying bills in a timely fashion speaks to how you do things in your life. It's not always easy to face these types of realities. There are so many other examples that I can use, but I believe the point has been made. It's not easy to face what we need to change or correct within our own lives. But it is necessary when building a brand foundation.

I am a firm believer that your brand's foundation must be firmly built in order for it to be sustained and succeed. This is really where integrity and building upon good relationships plays a pivotal role. Being haphazard about our associations is not good. I am in no way promoting a prejudicial approach but that of having a good choice and business sense for what can affect you in the long run.

What if you were a parent who had a budding child star who has breakout roles in the television commercial business? As offers are presented, you'd likely turn down an opportunity to work with a company promoting alcoholic beverages, especially if your goal is to promote a wholesome image for your child's brand. Doing something like that would not be good for business. Poor choices begat poor results. That is why so many people suffer severe blows or "letdowns" when trying to climb certain personal or career ladders. The first issue may be not having established a clear enough road map on how they want to achieve their goals, and the other may be compromising to try to attain a goal. Building on a foundation that is corrupt or unstable will not maintain a lasting building.

I'm on My Way . . .

Often, when a candidate wins the presidential election and takes on the role to lead a nation, in some fashion, they've been an understudy to their predecessors. There are two good reasons why a leader would want to study the actions of previous leaders: to know what worked and to learn what did not.

Times of culture and climate are always changing; therefore, what may have worked 50 years ago may still work or be quite obsolete. You must have the right perspective toward your area of focus. How many wars or recessions could have been avoided based on a conglomerate of decisions made?

Think of property development. There's a huge difference in creating a village versus a kingdom. The details can be as simple or as elaborate as the developer's vision. The quality of the materials used also directly impacts the quality of work. We know Rome was not built in a day, but we do know Rome was built. It took much labor, activity, and research to construct. In order to construct and finish the building of an entire city, much planning was required, with attention paid to details and consistency.

You Can't Be on again and off again When It Comes to Your Brand . . .

Every aspect of brand development will have twists and turns. You may experience some hits and misses, but you must have a *stick-to-it-ness*. Although this is not a word we generally use, it is highly effective in painting the picture that I want you to see. Another fitting word is *perseverance*.

Perseverance is tenacity. It is steadfastness, and in its simplest terms, plain old grit. Grit is described as courage and resolve. Perseverance is not something that is automatically transferable. The only way you'll get it is by overcoming difficulties, wading through life's challenges, and becoming an overcomer. What does an overcomer do? They focus and conquer.

One of the main outcomes of being focused is becoming a finisher. The only way to finish or achieve anything in life is by tackling all endeavors with our undivided attention. The key word is *undivided*. If you divide yourself up into too many areas to focus on, you cannot focus. Imagine a horse wearing blinders. These prevent the horse from looking to the left or to the right. The horse is forced to look straight-ahead. That is how we must be. Or consider when we spread ourselves *too thin*. No one can be everywhere and surely no one can do everything. *Focus* is when one targets his or her ability. This is when you put forth everything you have in a specific, concentrated effort; you give it your all.

Focus should lead to excellence. This is why it is one of the primary, if not the main, ingredient to building a great brand. I once worked for an organization whose motto was, "*Believing Excellence Is Attainable.*" The next organization I went on to work for owned a slightly different motto: "*Expecting Excellence Every Day.*" Both were pertinent to each of their causes, but if you examine them closely, they are two totally different approaches to the excellence message.

The first organization wanted the employees to shift their mind from where they were, to becoming one that acted on excellence, as to understand that excellence is an effort. This motto wanted one to realize that excellence could be reached; that it's doable. The second organization that used *Expecting Excellence Every Day* set the tone and conveyed the feel that nothing less than your very best would even be tolerated. This went beyond believing; it was the *I'm executing here!* There's no question what excellence looks like when you expect it. You're shooting way above the basics, but indeed, your endeavor is to go above and beyond.

Excellence Everywhere

Excellence must be a standard that encompasses not some, but *every* area of our life. Sometimes we like to address only certain areas of our lives, but leave other significant parts unattended. This may be due to internalized fears of the unknown. Some of those hurting areas or "messy" ones are way easier to sweep over or cover up. I'm the first to tell you there are times in my own life where I'd just rather ignore them than go through the "process" of it all. But truly, unless the mess is addressed (weaknesses, wounds, fears, etc.), they will affect the areas where our strength lies. Life is made up of several compartments and each and every one connects to the other. It's like a dresser. We store things in different spaces, but it's all a part of the same piece of furniture.

Consider a train and its many cars which make the whole. Each car is functional and is just as important as all the others. All train cars are intended to carry travelers safely. Each car will house different demographics of travelers. The young, the old, culturally diverse, etc. The goal is to get all traveling parts (people) safely to their destination. People are multidimensional and multifaceted. Imagine you are the train and each car represents a different function in your life. None can afford to choose to ignore any of the train cars, because each one of them is designed to carry out its own unique purpose or function.

The choice to address each area or compartment in our lives is critical to our overall growth, development, and ultimate success. At some point, those neglected areas will surface in another area at a time we can least afford them to.

For example, you might be an awesome entrepreneur, working long hours, making the sales, doing what it takes to get ahead. But let's imagine in doing so you fail to spend time with your spouse, children, or other loved ones. Or, let's say you don't take care of your physical and emotional well-being by not giving them the proper attention. You fail to exercise, eat right, or get a proper amount of rest. You may then end up suffering in all those areas respectively.

Setting one's self up with a vision for excellence must come from a holistic perspective which will allow one to have goals and dreams, necessary to achieve in all areas of one's life. I oftentimes think of the Olympic Games as I ponder on all of these traits and what goes into creating a "brand of champions." There is a great investment and amount of sacrifice that goes into competing on the Olympic level. The first step for any athlete to take is to identify his/her greatest talent or gift. Although many athletes may be able to perform well in multiple sports, they tend to perform well in one and have a greater passion and skill in one over all the others.

When I think of being multitalented in this way, the historic Jackie Robinson comes to mind and, once again, the all-time great Michael Jordan. Mr. Robinson is known by many as the first Negro (they were not called African American in those days) to play in the major leagues for baseball in the modern era. Few, however, know that he was also a varsity-lettered player for a total of four college sports. In addition to baseball, he ran track, played football, and basketball. A varsity letter is an award earned in the United States for excellence in school activities and signifies that its winner was a qualified varsity team member. This recognition was only awarded after a certain standard was met in the sport. Jackie Robinson even played tennis too.

Michael Jordan has been hailed as the best NBA player of all time by the NBA and by most sports enthusiasts on the planet. He also had a dual career in basketball and in baseball. I won't harp too much on his baseball career, although he did do well in the minor leagues. Michael is also considered one of the most successfully marketed figures in sports history. His brand marketing? In one word . . . explosive.

Just Do It!

Outside of his many accomplishments on the court, Michael Jordan has been hailed as king off the court as well by skyrocketing the brand of many name brand products. The brands are recognized through companies such as McDonald's to Nike to movies, and the list goes on. His Air Jordan signature shoe brand recently celebrated its thirtieth-year anniversary and is selling now more than ever. In 2014, he was named as the first billionaire NBA player in history. Can you imagine in his early years as a youth he was told by a coach that his basketball skills were *not* at NBA level? I'm so glad he didn't internalize those words. In September 2015, he was enshrined into the

FIBA Hall of Fame, the International Basketball Federation's governing body, and a few years earlier, in the Naismith Memorial Basketball Hall of Fame for his contributions as an individual to the sport and for his contributions on the United States Olympic Basketball Team.

Even as I mention this, I'm reminded of a colleague and friend whose daughter is one of the top 10 female water polo players on the high school level in the United States right now. Because of this young lady's talent and winnings, she's been recruited by some of the top colleges who house this particular sport's program, and she was able to secure a 4-year college scholarship at the close of her senior year. She is also now training rigorously for the pre-Olympic Trials. Projections predict that her talents have a strong chance to allow her to place for a spot in the future Olympics. But, for her, the hard work is just "now" beginning. You can't be named among the best without being the best.

Investing in training camps to practice and many other sacrifices are being made now in order for her to become the best while preparing to compete on this level. It took much resilience and endurance already to make it to this level. My friend is personally taking her daughter to the practices, committing her own time four consecutive evenings a week. This is where the "next" becomes the complete focus. The dawn of envisioning what the end result will be is on the horizon. When competing on this level, one must take on a global view in the sense of seeing and believing beyond the current conditions and sacrifices. This is the same way you must approach your personal brand. Condition your mind for such high goals to be excellent in the area that you are operating in.

One final thought I want you to take away is that excellence is surpassing goals you've set for yourself. Now that we've considered the professional sports athlete making it to Olympian heights, this is where I want you to see yourself . . . at the top of your game. These individuals have found something that they do well and are tapping into all areas of their talent to display it in its top form. They train tirelessly to prepare for various competitive situations. Even if what you are looking to achieve is not along the lines of an athletic nature, you can strive for the same mind-set in whatever endeavors you undertake.

Customer Service and the Crisis in American Culture

Among the many obvious crises rearing their ugly heads in the United States these days is that of how customers feel they are being treated by the very businesses that they choose to patronize. Based on the socioeconomic status of the consumer, the experience one is subject to is like night and day. "Money talks," an old term, implies that if you have money, you're treated one way, and those without are treated another. To a degree, that may be true, but the almighty dollar is not as powerful as it used to be in the marketplace. Many are now judged by the content of their persona, not the contents in their wallets. Even the rich and wealthy are not exempt from meeting the perceived obligations that having substantial amounts of money may bring.

Wrong Perceptions

You and I have likely had a life experience where we may have been looked down upon (a nicer way of saying *judged*) by our literal or perceived appearance (gender, race, and social class), perceived possessions (or in many instances, the number of zeros in our bank account), and the power or perceived personal "connections" we may have. I feel these behaviors by others lie at the root of most of the problems that lead to poor customer service.

Poor customer service is embedded in the fiber of our nation, and this crisis now appears to be everywhere. There are reports literally on a daily basis in the news outlets, from family members, friends, colleagues, you name it, of disappointment during a business transaction.

This problem lies in every industry and every sector. From retail to restaurants. From bankers to beauticians, our country is in need of a serious makeover. In some cases, I suggest a complete do over because the foundation was never built at the onset.

The deterioration of this area is causing grave damage to so many business and personal brands. Although good customer service may not be identified in writing when communicating a brand's mission, it is indeed a very core part of it. The mission of any organization sets out to clearly identify the goals, purpose, and work of any organization, all of which connect to some type of client profile.

Customer service is the vehicle that transports everything about your brand. It identifies the manner in which you do what you do. This concern affects so many aspects of any customer and business relationship. What is attributing to this crisis, however, can be up for great debate. When I recently posted my thinking on social media after being subject to a poorly handled business encounter, I received a great deal of feedback from my social media followers. The post simply read: *"America needs a customer service revolution. I think I'll start one, and I don't think I'm the only one that feels this way."* And, oh, did the responders chime in!

One commenter proposed that what currently lies in the thinking process of the "younger adults" and their concepts are much different than those who have gone before them. Others feel it's another group that's not so young, but too young to retire, and have been in a job way too long (i.e., city workers like teachers, public aid offices, unemployment offices, etc.). As a result, this deficit is causing catastrophic results on the front lines of many public or business entities.

> *"People are simply livid by what they are experiencing out in the general public face-to-face, on the phones via the call centers, you name it. This problem is affecting the masses."*
>
> —Consumer

One of the worst things in the world is to make someone feel unimportant when it comes to supporting you. No one should ever feel that your organization is okay with a customer or client taking their business or need for services elsewhere. Poor customer service completely impacts your brand and its ability to have staying power. Business owners must begin honing their staff on this because they are the greatest extension of a representation of their brand. Staff holds the key on how you represent the product or service to the world.

There are some customer service "essentials" that are mandatory. The basic greetings, whether in person or over the phone, should be, "Good morning," "Hello," or, "How may I help you?" The two words that many believe still go a long way in any customer-client transaction are "thank you." Instead, we're subjected to whatever they feel like throwing out at the time.

"How I feel" should be a minimal factor in a business setting. Too many employees tend to communicate "what they feel like doing" and "what they *don't* feel like doing." Just do it! I may not feel like getting up, but because I have commitments, I must. I've heard students sometimes convey how they like math, but they don't like reading. Or, they like reading, but they don't like math. Guess what I've had to tell them? Learning has little to do with what you feel or what you may or may not like. It has everything to do with what is being required of you, as a student. There are certain basic requirements of being a human being and for our role in American society.

Verbalizing emotions aren't necessary to get a job done. We all face difficulties or challenges. If they impede you from giving your best effort, talk to a reliable colleague or your manager.

Diversity all Around

One major concern that has surfaced is that many organizations must continue to maintain a certain level of sensitivity to a diverse clientele. Some people are not receptive to those who as aren't familiar to them. Sometimes this type of behavior is not necessarily being done on purpose, but regardless, it can be viewed by the recipient as disrespectful. When running any organization, it's always best to maintain an open mind. As the leader or business owner, you are always impacting the development of your brand, positively or negatively, whether you're trying to or not.

Sometimes your business or organization will gain support from unlikely patrons that are sometimes from places you would have never imagined. An online article and interview with an executive in the Chicago White Sox organization stated how some of the actors in the blockbuster movie *Straight Outta Compton* were walking billboards for some of their sports gear. The organization was happy with that. They'd received recognition and product sales that they hadn't even planned for. Everyone in business must continue to realize that the customer base is the backbone of the business.

The Internal Factor: How Poor Customer Service Affects a Business Brand

The factor lies in one simple word: *choice*. Because there are so many choices for just about every product or service sector nowadays, a wise builder must be in the business of just that . . . building.

Everyone Is a Customer . . .

I tell people you are always either a customer or you are a potential customer. How many times has an owner been unaware that customers or potential customer were dissatisfied? I had a recent experience at a nail spa. One main reason that I became interested in even going there was based on their advertisement. On paper, the experience that was promised seemed to be one that I would not want to pass up. So I purchased the special coupon voucher. I was quite interested in learning more about their services and because of my excitement, I shared information about my purchase. People were expecting to hear from me about the experience. Some were poised to make an appointment. Even before I stepped one foot in the door, I had made future plans to revisit already.

The receptionist showed minimal to no enthusiasm for my presence when I walked up to the counter. At minimum, I should've been asked if that was my first time visiting by the individual checking me in. When I presented the voucher, that should have been another signal to prompt her to think that maybe I was someone new. Also, the fact that this was a special "promotional" package should have also given a hint that I was a first-time customer and should have been handled as such.

On the surface, her attire was neat and professional. I would give her a high rating in being well dressed. But what happened through her actions let me know that there was an obvious disconnect somewhere in either experience or training. I concluded that it was mostly her personality that negatively affected her dealings with me. Our personality is part of who we are as individuals, affected by our prior life experiences. But the standards of a work environment do not always accommodate what is considered personal. It should be professional.

The couple of key words hiding in the word *personality* are "personal" and "person." In professional settings, there is less room for a person's personal issues. That's why it's called *work*. Personal represents intimacy or exclusivity; there should be a lid placed on how much of that is allowed to spill over into our professional working situations. Doing so can make things become quite uncomfortable. A business is always a business, first.

Things that are of a personal nature in your life should remain guarded. As a matter of fact, because they are "personal," it is important to know what to share and what not to share, and above all, whom to share it with. There is one thing to be transparent, but there is another to be downright over the top.

When it comes to business, less of our person should be a part of the picture or equation in the overall scope of things. It doesn't take great insight to determine that people should detect a certain level of pleasantness about us in our professional dealings with customers when doing our jobs, no matter our role in the company. A poor attitude should always remain on the outside of the door.

Why Customers Walk

You can't always control what you become subject to, but you can take control of what's permitted. Sometimes, customers walk out due to their initial impressions in a transaction that may have occurred because of poor communication with one of the employees. There are countless opportunities around the world to make an impact on customers. There should be thousands of ways to ensure that customers become returning customers. Not one customer should say he or she is not returning due to a lack of services provided.

Never leave a bad taste in someone's mouth when it comes to any type of business dealings with you or from those who are associated with your brand.

Customers may come in with attitudes, and that's something to be prepared for. If they leave, it should be because their need could not be met—not because you ran them away. There should never be a time when a customer leaves and feels that you didn't want them to return. There is a chance that a relationship on any level may no longer be able to meet the needs of the client, and parting ways becomes mandatory, but it should never be because of something your organization did.

Our reputation must be able to speak without us ever needing to say a word ourselves. Once those connections or established alliances are in place, our reputation must go before us in a positive light. A good name speaks volumes in every industry. Some circles are quite small, and word of mouth travels faster than a major marketing announcement.

A year ago I applied for a particular program, and I was not chosen. I had spent a great deal of time building up to it, expecting a positive result. I had to invest in this process by paying fees, gathering documents, writing, requesting written recommendations, and much follow-up. I stayed in constant contact with the individual in charge of the program every step of the way. This individual was a tremendous source of information and answered all of my questions. I met all of the deadlines for paperwork, etc., meeting all necessary requirements. When I finally received notification that the decision was made and that I did not make the final cut, one would think that I would have been super disappointed.

Truthfully, I could thank them for turning me down. Though I thought this would be a great opportunity, in actuality, it was not where my heart was leading me to go with my life. The feedback was immediate and brutal. I gained something more valuable from the process. I now consider this person whom I'll refer to as Dr. T., one of my professional mentors.

In everyday life and business, there is always potential to make a connection. Even if I, as a consumer, may not be a candidate for your products or services, maybe I know someone who is. Therefore, keep an open mind and a positive perspective. Have you ever located a potential service provider, but after interacting with them, you realize that they may just not have been right for you? Yet, those interactions may not always have been dead ends either. Sometimes as a result of those communications, you may receive referrals and even recommendations which will get you exactly what you need.

Take a moment to reflect on the people who impacted you the most. Some people, when you think about them, bring a smile to your face because of their great impact on you. There are people that are just like that in all of our lives. One of my main desires is that I want people who have any dealings with me to have those same positive feelings.

The most impact that anyone can make in any situation is to first make a connection (showing how one can relate) and a model ("how to do" what it is you want to do). This creates a live and a visible example. The core of the mission, vision, and values needs to be clear to those who have the responsibility of serving customers as front liners (not just them, but *especially* them). The front liners are who I would call your true believers. They will convey and convince others of your message or product. They know and understand what the mission, vision, and core values are to represent to those coming from the outside. They also have a strong passion and belief system that undoubtedly shines through. These are the folks who will come in early and stay late without missing a beat. This group aspires to "do the work" to show others that it can be done. They aspire to become protégés of their leader.

There is so much power given to the front liners. You are your front line. And if you're working for a business or organization, you are *their* front line. The expectation is that the managers of these individuals are charged with keeping abreast of the happenings among this critical mass or group.

Keep in mind that some business owners or leaders, depending on the nature of their role in the organization, may not always get an opportunity to correspond with those representing or interacting with the customers of the business on the front lines. Most work settings and circumstances don't always allow owners to be physically present 24/7, so the leadership model they create is a critical component to its success. Some businesses allow for ground-level interactions of business owners with their customers, whereas others are set up and require more removed roles.

You should take the most intricate care of those who are your arch-supporters. There should be a uniform plan in place to train those who are the front line or face of your business.

With the amount of experience that I've garnered over the years, I made a decision the day of the spa incident to not allow what happened with this young lady to be the sole factor to formulate my entire opinion of the business. I could have chosen to walk at this point, but I decided to wait and see if things would get better. Unfortunately, things got progressively worse. I decided that I would seek to meet with the owner in an attempt to have a very friendly but professional conversation in a manner that would bring understanding to the situation.

So after my Saturday appointment, I went back on that Monday at lunchtime. Near the entrance, a young lady outside appeared to be taking a break. I asked her if she worked for the spa, and she stated that she did. I then asked for the owner's name and asked if she was there. When I walked through those doors that day, the young lady who had spearheaded this entire scenario had a shocked expression. It was as if she didn't know what to think or how I might describe her behavior from days earlier. One of the stylists came over to ask if she could help, but I told her that I was good and that I was waiting to see the manager.

The general rule of thumb I learned over the years is . . . when sharing not-so-pleasant news about anything, first start by incorporating two positive things before ever mentioning anything negative.

The owner finally came after servicing *her* client and approached me. I must now also address the fact that most all of the polish on my fingernails had chipped off within 24 hours of the first visit. That was definitely another issue altogether that needed be addressed. I told her how friendly my actual nail tech had been on that Saturday, but the problem was with the product itself not lasting on my nails and the receptionist's treatment. Here, though, was the first problem—the owner could barely speak English. I had not predicted this to happen. So, she had to bring over an employee who spoke English to help interpret what I wanted to convey to her. Unfortunately, it ended up being the very employee whom I had mentioned a little earlier that had asked if I needed assistance at the onset.

Although this made for an "interesting" circumstance, I relayed my experience to the manager. Initially, I felt slightly uncomfortable at first speaking because this meeting was in plain view of the involved parties. I felt like I was telling my story to the entire salon. The person whom I was referring to in my complaint was actually sitting at the front desk a few feet away. I'm certain she could hear everything we were saying.

The manager listened intently and seemed to be holding on to every single word. She seemed to become remorseful about my experience and was apologetic throughout my sharing. It appeared that she was clear on what had transpired and not once did she choose to defend any behaviors or make excuses for her staff, which I did find somewhat refreshing. The manager offered to provide me with a full refund or the opportunity to have another manicure after looking at my chipped fingernail polish. We seemed to come to a mutual understanding that I would remain a customer and return to have my manicure corrected. I asked them to fill me in for an appointment for the next day in the early afternoon hours. In that moment with all the "warm and fuzzies," I just knew this could be a brand-new start in the right direction. I left feeling good about giving this place another chance.

When I arrived home later on that evening I found that I had a previously scheduled commitment the following day that would conflict with my new appointment at the spa. I called the spa, but they had gone for the day. I called again the next day, reached the receptionist, and explained the situation. I then told her that I would contact them later to reschedule. After I had finished my other appointment, I checked my phone. I had a message from the spa. The message stated that the owner saw that I had canceled my appointment and that I *had to call back and select a time within 24 hours or I would lose my ability to get the services redone altogether*. I was like, "huh?"

So I called to speak to the owner who was unavailable to try to understand the "new" problem here. Not only was she telling me I had to come on her terms, she was also limiting me to the option of being serviced by the same individual that had performed the first services. Oh, but it gets even more interesting when I checked to see what time the nail technician had available. The woman had little-to-no openings to offer in such a short window of time. My thoughts were, *Why didn't any of this come up yesterday?* No one conveyed any time restrictions then. On top of that, as the afternoon went on, the manager didn't return my call. Now they were adding insult to injury.

When I called later that evening, the manager had gone for the day, but the receptionist informed me that she had received my message and that she would not be making *any* changes. The only option I was given was to come on their terms or lose my money. So now, along with throwing me into an entirely new dynamic, they were penalizing me by forcing me to choose inconvenient time slots on a day that would not work.

After processing all that had transpired since Saturday, I told her I would be seeking a refund because, obviously, there was no interest in keeping my business. I contacted the company that had played the middle man in providing the deal and lodged a formal complaint. The latter company not only refunded the money that I'd used for the purchase of the voucher, they also gave an additional instant credit toward future coupon purchases. Now, who do you think I'll be doing business with in the future?

A good business values excellent customer service. This is not always simply equated to dollars and cents. Sometimes, the greatest values are that of sharing ideas and solutions and being able to make amicable agreements. All are equally important.

7

BRAND PROTECTION

To Share or Not to Share?

Too much information is put out on social media platforms nowadays, whether in celebrity reports or from everyday people communicating about their personal lives.

My Brand Is Beautiful

Have you ever noticed that everything in our society has been set up to meet a particular need? From hospitals to churches, from cabs to smartphones, the list goes on. Functionality comes when it's determined where we fit in the bigger scope of things. For example, a hospital is an establishment that has all components of a corporation. There is the medical component of service professionals who are in place to meet the immediate needs of those seeking medical care—doctors, nurses, CNAs, EMTs, maintenance workers, cooks, receptionists, morgue workers, chaplains, security personnel, parking attendants, pharmaceutical vendors, etc. This group of staff is set in place to meet the basic need of functionality.

But there are so many other components. You have the legal team. The extensive amount of legal work that must go into running a hospital is astounding. Simply referring to the paperwork or hospital documents are, in most cases, sensitive legal documents that hospitals must maintain for patient care and for possible litigation. Hospitals are also entities that are most susceptible to lawsuits due to cases of malpractice. They must take on a defense role (defending their doctor teams and hospital community) and an offense role (safeguarding the potentials or unknowns), especially when it's hard to tell if an unfortunate incident is within the realm of human error or an "Act of God."

The finance and insurance entity is the heart of the entire operation. Getting paid is the headliner in most instances whenever a service is rendered. Then there are foundations, collections, etc. Investment in the equipment is of the highest priority because, in some way, the equipment's use is tied back to a life. Hospitals must remain on the cutting edge of technological breakthroughs in medicine. The way the world evolves is to determine who can advance or improve on existing techniques or procedures.

The difference is all in the packaging; the brand. What makes you choose one hospital over another? What makes you seek out one specialist versus the one your health plan imposed on you? What makes you buy tires from a tire shop versus purchasing them from the dealer that sold you your vehicle? What makes you drive across town to go to a certain hairstylist and pass a dozen other hair salons before you get there?

You can bank on the fact that the way one is being treated has just as much to do with those choices, combined with the benefit of whatever the product or service that is being provided. Another factor that greatly impacts any business is customer "word of mouth" referrals about your business. What better reference than that of another customer who has experienced what your business has to offer? Publicity by word of mouth can be one of greatest marketing tools for your business, *if* it has and maintains a good reputation. This can also be one of your worst nightmares should consumers start to identify unfavorable businesses because of encounters with those representing you and your brand in some capacity.

Poorly orchestrated customer interactions can lead to the untimely death of a business if the root of the problem is not resolved. There are two main issues that, although should be very simple and clear, are factors that would affect any business's customer relationships. They are *poor* customer service and/or a *lack* of customer service. You may say poor and lack are one and the same; however, these terms do have a distinct difference. Sometimes a few moments can cause the type of damage that can take years to repair. Sometimes reputations can be completely destroyed. Being very protective of the things that are valuable to you, not only in personal relationships, but in our business relationships, is key.

A real pet peeve of mine is making a purchase and placing the money in the cashier's hand, only to have that cashier return that money by laying it on the counter. That is very disrespectful. This is one of my main customer service no-no's. I typically will, in a pleasant way, let that individual know politely what I expect. It's interesting though how sometimes people look at you like you're speaking a foreign language.

There is a song that was written some years ago and I can clearly remember the hook. It was a duet, and the part that sticks out in the verse is "Where is the love? Where is the love? Where is the love?" It's repeated several times, rotating between singers. For some reason, these lyrics seem always make me think of something other than love in the traditional sense of the word. When I hear this, I think of the term *customer service,* and where did it go? What happened to the love of caring about how you treat a business, or its matters, to the extent that whatever is happening that will affect patrons is taken to heart?

Sometimes when out and about in such places as service agencies, restaurants, or retail stores, the personnel who work there determine how they are going to interact based on what they see. There are some benefits/amenities you will gain access to and others that will be denied to you based on a person's comfort level with you. People choose to respect or dismiss what they see.

When I think of poor customer service, it as an intentional behavior by an employee, disregarding the company's principles or core values. In other words, they know what to do and how to do it, but allow various factors to get in the way of what they were hired to do. There are a myriad of influences that can cause interference so that an individual will not do what he should. To behave in this matter intentionally is absolutely unacceptable. In doing my research of declining loyalty in the workplace, I recently located a great read titled *Declining Employee Loyalty: A Casualty of the New Workplace* (author unknown) which stated some very interesting findings on why people don't seem to adhere to commitments in the workplace. The article stated:

"The loyalty levels for employees in various working situations have been on a steady decline. If loyalty is defined as being faithful to a cause, ideal, custom, institution or product, then there seems to be a certain amount of infidelity in the workplace these days" as quoted from Wharton's School online business journal *The Know*. The results, according to the article from the 2012 MetLife's 10th Annual Survey, focuses on the employee response to benefits, trends, and attitudes, which indicated that employee loyalty was at a 7-year low at the time the report was taken.

> *"One in three employees,"* the survey says, *"plans to leave his or her job by the end of the year. According to a 2011 Careerbuilder.com report, 76% of full-time workers, while not actively looking for a new job, would leave their current workplace if the right opportunity came along. Other studies show that each year, the average company loses anywhere from 20% to 50% of its employee base."*
>
> Source~http://knowledge.wharton.upenn.edu

Avoiding "Brand Busters." Brand-New Management

Working hard to build something, then to see it be torn down in an instant, can become one of the most disheartening experiences ever. The word *build* alone resonates something that will take time. The actuality of perfection in a brand is not a reality; however, the investment to make it what it is, does. It's admirable to have great intent to remain in a grand brand space, but humans do have mishaps. Certain behaviors can put our brand at risk. There are actions that do not complement us, and these actions must be controlled when working to guard our brand. Some behaviors that threaten to surface in our lives for various reasons don't need an extensive explanation. Sometimes, you can simply be having a bad day. That may be true, but let me explain why excuses should not be accepted. People must learn how to identify our limitations. I'll use this example.

You may wake up not feeling well on a particular morning, but it's one of the busiest days of the week for your company. You don't want to seem like you're a slacker, but you're not up to doing your best, and you go into work anyway. Then the worst happens . . . You have an altercation with a customer. Now, because you aren't feeling well, you are not able to function at your best, and after a few interactions with the internal and/or external customers, you've compromised yourself. Why? People are coming into an unfair situation at the onset and are clueless about what you're dealing with. You are not even your normal self. Now, what was intended to be a noble gesture has turned into a chaotic circumstance that could have been avoided had different decisions been made—all because you didn't gauge the fact that being ill would impact your functionality. Utilizing a sick day may have prevented much less duress on the entire scenario. Benefit days are there for a reason—so you can give the proper attention to your health concerns.

Let me be clear, I'm not condoning the type of behavior of those who take off for every little sniffle or sneeze. There's a ton of people who abuse their benefit days to the point it puts an unnecessary burden on coworkers and the business. You know when whatever health challenge you're experiencing is mild enough to work on through it, or severe enough to impact everyone else (flu, colds, other contagious symptoms). It's actually all right to take care of you. But staying out late every night, not getting proper rest or eating the right foods or exercising properly all lead up to your being worn out and unproductive. People not taking true care of their own well-being seems to be one of the greatest self-neglect trends in today's workforce. I know this is partially due to the competitive nature of our society as it relates to climbing the career ladder.

Many people have adopted a "whatever it takes" frame of thinking when it comes to advancing in their career, and they are doing themselves and everyone else a disservice in the process.

Another behavior many display is a fear of losing their job; therefore, they self-sacrifice. I have known people who've had major medical procedures done, but because of the fear their job would be filled by someone else, they have come back to work before being fully healed, recovered, and released by their doctor. I've seen this happen over several occasions in my career. One time, however, my coworker lost her life due to this behavior. She had blood clots in her body and risked coming to work prematurely after major surgery. She would always be one of the first to arrive at work. This particular morning, she was found on the steps of the company, unresponsive. She came to work because she didn't want to be replaced in her job. There are no winners when this type of thinking persists. In the bigger picture, these actions that may seem selfless, but on the surface, they are much more costly to your brand.

8

BRANDTASTIC

Many businesses or personal brands can go from being virtually unknown to becoming an all-out success. Food icons like McDonald's and Kentucky Fried Chicken (KFC) are great examples of breakout food chain brands.

> *"If I had a brick for every time I've repeated the phrase Quality, Service, Cleanliness and Value, I think I'd probably be able to bridge the Atlantic Ocean with them."*

This statement by Ray Kroc, the one who developed McDonald's into a billion-dollar franchise, says a great deal. It means that he had more than just a framework for him and his staff to live by that went well beyond their products. He wanted to ensure that by keeping the core foundation, McDonald's would become a part of the food industry as a thriving force. He did not want to be limited or boxed into one location of service.

Ray Kroc began his journey at the age of 52 in 1955. That alone sends the message that it's never too late to launch a dream. Many in our current generation would consider 52 to be on the older end of the spectrum, but I'm glad that he and Colonel Sanders—founder KFC at the age of 62—didn't allow age to deter them from their dreams.

Ray observed two brothers, Dick and Mac McDonald, operating their restaurant. Because the method they employed seemed to show so much potential with such a limited number of offerings on its menu, Ray pursued the permission from the McDonald brothers to revamp systems of the restaurant. By allowing the focus to remain on the *quality* of the product as well as the *speed* in producing the product, this would become the truest origin of "fast" food. Ray wanted this idea showcased on a much-larger scale, so he took this model to the masses through replication (burgers, fries, and milkshakes done in a certain way with the same formula) while keeping the same signature look and taste. He convinced the brothers of the idea of going national, so the birth of the McDonald's franchise came to fruition.

Six years after meeting the McDonald brothers, Ray not only had exceeded the initial plan, but he was now in a position to purchase exclusive rights to the company's name. In just 3 years' time, the company sold its 100-millionth hamburger. Just as McDonald's began humbly, KFC grew in strides from the determination of a single thought.

KFC's history is similar in that the idea started with just one person with a vision, Colonel Sanders. He had a recipe and a dream to see his idea go all over the world. The concept came at a time when people were struggling during the Great Depression. Colonel Sanders wanted families to still have access to quality, affordable meals. He initially started with one restaurant where he worked hard to perfect his craft and product. Just like Ray Kroc, Colonel Sanders sought opportunities to franchise, and many moons later, this powerful story is stronger now more than ever with over 18,000 KFC outlets in 115 countries and territories around the world.

As adults become mature, it takes that much more focus and tenacity to move forward in order to not become more set in our way of thinking. This makes more of a challenge to *just do it* for some. Everyone has a different biological makeup or DNA, but some people at certain points in their life don't want to make drastic changes, whether it be a career move, a geographic move, etc. Maturing adults start to become more of settlers in their ways.

I don't have to mention the brand imagery that comes to mind with both of these companies. Probably while I told the story, your tummy grumbled or you might have put the book down long enough to grab something to eat. Maybe those golden arches, the red base and white letters came to mind, or an image of that silver-white hair, glasses, and thin tie. For years, both companies have done their jobs to make sure their brand has a long-lasting presence.

McDonald's founded the Ronald McDonald Houses and Care Mobiles. The KFC Foundation supports the goals of its employees by providing funding for them to complete various aspects of their own education goals. The idea of giving back is already quite remarkable, but to found an organization that gives back solely to those who have supported you in achieving your goals and dreams, that is one of the greatest returns on investments.

9

TAKE NOTHING
FOR GRANTED

ife is all about managing what you have, and managing well. You may not have the right amount of resources to start, but appreciating what you already have and working with it is a great point of preparation.

My very first car was a two-door hatchback Hyundai Excel (ironic that it included the word *excel*, which is derived from the word *excellence*). Knowing what I know today about appreciation versus depreciation, I would've driven that car until the wheels fell off. I had a ridiculously low car note of just $164 for that vehicle. Wow, to have those days back would be a dream. You would have thought I owned a high-end luxury vehicle like a Rolls-Royce or a Mercedes-Benz because I treated that apple-red beauty of a Hyundai so well. I kept it super clean inside and out all year-round, as if it was my "home away from home."

What you do with the little you have is an indicator of what you will do with much more. For example, if you can't care for whatever make or model vehicle you currently have right now, it will be highly unlikely that you'll treat your "dream" car any different.

Sometimes, you can tell how clean a person keeps their home based on the way they handle the upkeep of their car. It's unlikely that someone would maintain an immaculate home, then drive around with their car care down in the dumps. My father taught me to always be timely in addressing maintenance issues for my vehicles. I was taught that everything is a blessing. In many instances, the belief system typically trickles into many other areas of our lives which affects our brand.

Because you are your brand, the greatest care you can give is to yourself . . . body, mind, and soul. I believe if one does their very best toward taking good care of things entrusted into your care, surely one day you will be given the opportunity to move on to something better (and in this example, maybe a more luxurious vehicle). I am thankful to have been raised by parents who exemplified the principles that I'm attempting to convey in this book. My parents were always consistent with their own beliefs of how they cared for their family and the workings of their personal affairs.

10

Post with a Purpose; Platform Building

Perception is everything when building your brand. The way you are viewed determines who will follow your message in whatever form it's told. When posting on social media, there should always be a purpose at the center of why you create certain posts. There was a bit of advice given to me years ago by a mentor that is still relevant.

Never write anything that everyone can't read and never record anything that everyone can't listen to.

If you're willing to put it out there, then you must be willing to accept the potential reactions to what you've exposed in your life. Once it's out there in some instances, you "literally" cannot take it back. So take care in this aspect of your brand.

There is some information out there for everyone to benefit from. The key, however, is not to take information from everyone, but to try to determine who has shown proven results in your area of need. Get references, do the legwork. You cannot afford to become lax or settle for not knowing what's necessary in this area of branding.

A certain level of credence should be given to your personal safety and of those around you. Posting too much information can become detrimental if it falls into the wrong hands. There's identify theft for one. There are Internet prowlers who simply mean us no good.

Since employers are now using Facebook and other social media outlets to verify potential candidates before hiring, how you're represented on those mediums is ultra important. Posts that can be considered racially, sexually, and religiously charged, or profanity, can also prevent employment opportunities. Consider how this may affect you in the long run. Grammar and spelling also directly impact your representation of yourself when writing on social media. Write so that what you've written actually makes sense to the reader. Think, *am I clearly communicating the message that I want to go out in this post?* Do not to send out messages that show others in a negative light.

<H1>Distractions, Distractions, Detractions</H1>

I love the way that the world of social media has enabled many to connect together who might, otherwise, not do so. I love the fact that I have been able to reconnect with classmates and distant family members. I have honestly gotten to know some blood relatives better as a result of platforms like Facebook. I think anything used for the right purpose and in moderation can be beneficial, but if used in overkill mode, can be harmful.

Leave the gossip to the magazines. The length some of these organizations will go to "get a story" or "spill the dirt" on someone is disheartening. I believe that truth is important, but the motivation behind telling that truth is even more important. Remember that you should remain credible in what you post because, in the end, you wouldn't want those tables turned. I am all for progression in the digital age and when it comes to technological advancement, but some things have become downright intrusive as they relate to our personal lives. As a consenting adult, you reserve the right to share your business, but consider the consequences of doing so.

I love technology and social media. For me, it has been a godsend. News, both in the media and about friends and loved ones, can come immediately just because I happened to log on at that time. I've been contacted by colleagues (present and former), distant relatives, and grade-school classmates via social media platforms. I use my access too many times networking and making connections to information that is readily accessible. So the platform does have it benefits, but be disciplined.

Never respond to an e-mail while angry or you may regret it. The rule of thumb is to sleep on it before writing a response. Give your mind a chance to calm down while considering all sides of a situation. If there is something about what you put together that is going to make you ashamed down the road, don't post it. Words cannot be taken back, especially if they have been released into the cyber world.

I have witnessed many things that I would consider inappropriate on social media. Some language, pictures, videos, and advertisements I've seen have been offensive. Social media is like anything else; you can use it in a positive, useful manner, or the opposite. I think it's important to know *why* you're using social media. Be conscious of who is able to see the content you're posting; public, friends, friends of friends, etc. I can't expect everyone to think like me, but the wonderful thing that it brings to the consumer is choice . . . to share or not to share much.

Nowadays, police officers and other law enforcement manage online criminal investigation systems where they access social media to help in their research for criminal cases. What's more, they are finding success because people post so much of their thinking and activities. Not that I'm thinking you're considering a life of crime or anything like that, but the point I'm making is when online, you have to be smart and strategic with your brand and its presence on social media.

I love chiming in on certain discussions, interacting in a positive manner. Let's not forget that social media IS about being *social*—not psychotic. If you expect to be taken seriously, and you should want to be, your personal brand is something that you will want to strongly consider protecting fearlessly.

Whether intentional or not, people decide subconsciously right after an encounter with a person, what their opinion is going to be of them. Whether direct or indirect (i.e., telephone, e-mail, social media communications, etc.), whether completely justified or not. This activity may be one of the most underestimated assumptions that weigh so much on decisions that affect our everyday world.

Brand Reach

Communication is the key to building and maintaining a lasting brand.

You will not be able to reach everyone with your message, because everyone may not be your market, but for those that you are intending to impact, you don't want to be tainted by things that are within your control. Your goal is to ensure that you are focused on having a great level of clarity in order to remain in a posture to effectively and strongly impact those you are intending to reach. It is critical to realize that we cannot always predict the exact outcome of everything. That is the nature of living (the "life" factor), and in our humanity, those factors in life will involve many hits and misses.

Most people struggle with acceptance (at different levels, of course). It must be considered that everyone is at a different stage and age of their lives, and your message may not be for a particular group. Those you are supposed to interact with will gravitate to your work in a great way.

One of the best and key ways in getting your message out is through exemplar communication. In today's world, communication comes in many forms: verbal, visual, written, and directly from those you are set to impact the most . . . people. Each of these mediums is equally important in its own critical function. Although the format in communication may vary, you want to ensure you are relaying a consistent message in presentation and in quality. That is why brand checkers must be in place. Develop a system of checkpoints to ensure that your brand is protected. Whatever the amount manpower you have on staff or if you're riding fairly thin (i.e., just you), there should be people and/or processes identified to make this happen on a consistent basis.

Don't be afraid to make mistakes, but do be willing to potentially count up a great cost to the choices that are made. So it is indeed of the utmost importance to have clarity, a clear focus, and wisdom when building a brand.

11

A BRAND-NEW YOU

As a man thinks . . .

One key organizational tip I live by is . . . Everything has a home (someplace that it should go). When you brand something mentally, it becomes a "permanent" thought in your mind, and that thought is stored somewhere. In just dealing with the aspect of how one looks at himself or herself, this will also include how one views others.

People must learn to take the liberty to determine exactly where to put or compartmentalize thoughts in the most accurate "genre" or "group" in our thinking. In other words, when contact is made with people, there are multiple dimensions of where our opinions can take us as far as their brand is concerned or how they are representing themselves.

In my case, an unsuspected diagnosed condition that needed to be addressed and financial challenges arose. These situations affected my collegiate journey and forced me to stop taking classes for a year. I soon was back on the fast track to finish, and I did.

At the start of my career, I received various impressions of the companies where I applied. I needed to ensure that the vision and visionary had an important trait: a mind to expand and a willingness to support those who were supporting their vision. It's a horrible feeling to work for a place that has no intention of going beyond where they currently exist.

What was very important to me was to feel that I was going into an organization that had me in mind as they were building. The organization had to be about expansion and professional growth, and that even with thousands of employees, I would have the opportunity to grow. I had to have the sense that the team was actually growing together. Back then, and even now, this is referred to as "climbing the corporate ladder." In my naiveté and plans to take over the world, (yes, you read that right!), the reality was that some of those people who hired me did not have that same picturesque view of the world that I had. I am a dreamer. Putting youth, dreams, and the tool of education with it, I really felt unstoppable. Although that was my thought pattern (perceived reality), it was not necessarily how others felt about things. They just weren't as vested as I was in my future. Even more so, upon entering the workforce, I was taken aback by the dark reality of human nature, and individuals used underhanded methods to get what they wanted.

People were so focused on getting to the top with no regard for company loyalty, team, becoming qualified, and putting in time. I was now introduced to the games (of politics) that people played. Some thought getting on the good side of the manager while throwing you under the bus was the way. Some felt doing their job while cross-training for another was the solution.

After toiling with my own humanity and purpose in life and experiencing a number of tremendous ups and downs, I made the leap of faith to move into a new career. Now, I just said that, but it surely didn't happen just like that. There was a lot of pain, counsel, soul-searching, prayer, and research that, all put together, led me into the education profession. I was now a career changer, and that would take some rebranding.

People will always have their take on who you can become or what you are capable of doing, but it's really all up to you. When you work for most organizations, you are usually being compensated for what you "bring to the table" as far as skill set and experience, especially in the corporate industry/setting. As my own personal experiences increased after years of working in various capacities, I can recall hearing manager-mentors say things like, "Oh, she would never fit in here" or "I feel they're not right for that position." How subjective or political is that? Keep in mind, ideally, you are being hired to meet a need and to help further the mission or vision of the organization. But somewhere along the way, based on the power allocated to the hands of managers and executives, *they* actually hold the key to your future; thus, the corporate politics begin. People start "cozying" up to the bosses or start tearing down each other just to get ahead in the game. That's right, your life and future turn into a big old game. Whatever happened to the belief that, if hired, the expectation is somehow what you know or can do will aid in meeting the goals there, and that's what they really want in an employee?

In establishing clearly identifiable objectives, required skills and a purposeful plan are also key. Doing the preparation on the front end and having the necessary resilience on the back end to forge through all obstacles will get you on the path to your own life's journey. Nothing will ever replace working hard toward your dreams and being prepared. But in the midst of it all, you must be flexible and accept change—especially when things do not go the way you have planned. A mind-set of a positive image or message from the organization, and an opportunity for advancement for those committed to their vision was nonnegotiable whenever I took on any new employment opportunity.

Strategic defined: "relating to the identification of long-term or overall aims and interests and the means of achieving them."

I've always had a vision of where I wanted to go. So when I was determined to make the career switch to the field of education, these thoughts transferred. I had to know when taking a position that I could advance further if I chose to by taking the necessary steps to do so as communicated by the organization during the interview process. I would refer to this as the "promotion plan."

Most people by nature do not like ongoing change. Change, however, is inevitable. It is important to realize that change must be embraced when dealing with your brand. There has to be a willingness to adapt to what is needed, when needed.

It was the opportunities that led me to believe that I could bring value, and more importantly, that I had something to offer which was indeed a testament to the way that these organizations positioned or branded themselves.

More companies in previous generations in our society were able to hold on to employees for the long haul. In the workforce, there was more of a longevity mind-set. People would stay out of a sense of loyalty and what seemed to be a stable environment. What did they have then that companies don't portray now? Most people will only stay on a job if they know they can receive top dollar or a top post. Otherwise, they will continue to move on. The typical employee now has strict loyalty to meeting his or her own needs. That employee will stay there as long as circumstances are right for them. If and when the grass looks greener, they have no problem bailing.

In other words, previously, when you took a job, you were considering it for the long haul, and if you played your cards right, you could be there until retirement. Although raised in this era, I didn't totally adopt this type of thinking. And it's a good thing that I didn't. Today, it's an employer's market—and in some sectors, the employers are making it clear that employees are expendable.

I can think of my college experience as I was pursuing my under-graduate studies. Because I had chosen to attend school locally, for some reason, in my mind, going to a state university that had thousands of students was going to bring a level of prestige.

That first day on campus was a complete disaster. Imagine being one of over 25,000 students on a university campus and not knowing a single soul. Imagine the confusion of not understanding how college lectures were run. Not to mention, classes with over 200 people, and the professor not ever knowing you from Adam, or Eve, for that matter. I became so overwhelmed that I prayed and cried. Thankfully, I was able to locate another school that had a completely different profile and was more conducive to what I needed.

Unfortunately, people judge us by our appearance. Most people that we come into contact with for the very first time, after only a few short moments, have already, in some way, placed us into some type of category. Some insensitive and very sick stereotypical people have taken this to a whole other level. By that, I mean, based on the mere color of one's skin, gender, or some other factor. It should not be normal to think in this manner.

I am speaking more to the point of you as an individual being the very best you can be and getting into the intentional habit of being that *all the time*. Being the best you involves multiple facets of who you are (body, mind, and soul).

You are your own walking/talking billboard, the best advertisement, and a one-person marketing campaign every single day of your life. Nowadays, so much emphasis is being placed on the *exterior*. Competition is extremely fierce on all fronts, so you need to be "spot-on." The *initial* impression in many cases can become the *final* impression. It's not about having the most expensive things necessarily, but it is about keeping the things that you have at their best.

Have you ever met someone that seemed to have it all together on the outside, but as soon as they opened their mouth, you realized how tainted they were inside? As I mentioned earlier, there is a great emphasis on the outside, and the presence of the person. I have seen some cases where someone may judge a person based on their appearance, but because they had such a great heart and personality, that overshadowed everything else. This is not a campaign to be shallow, but to be the best. I believe that when the focus is on becoming exceptional in your area of expertise, then becoming the total package in that area holistically should be the goal.

The Power of Words . . .

I'm learning more and more to this very day how pivotal words are to the quality of our existence and how words have much power to determine who we are becoming. In doing so, I have also realized the importance of monitoring what I say. Not only is it critical to watch what *you* say, it's just as important to monitor what's being *said to you*. Words are so powerful and are often internalized—even more so, if they are not positive.

There are aspects of simply "living life" that are completely out of your control that seem to make things spiral out of control. Many times, these situations "pop up," and you can be easily moved off your charted course. And these particulars can cause us to have setbacks along our journey.

My first exposure to college expectations rolled around while still a senior in high school. Because I was having much success in "high" level English Language Arts classes in high school over the course of the first 3 years academically, in my senior year, I was offered the opportunity to take two college level English courses being offered by the local community college right on my high school campus. Upon successful completion, these two English classes were allowed to transfer as college coursework toward the completion of prerequisites at the local community college. I was basically given a head start on my college experience.

Although not my initial plan, I went on to continue my studies after high school at this same community college. I did this for a couple of reasons: first, my parents had clearly communicated to me early on in high school that they would not be able to afford to assist in paying for any college expenses, specifically tuition. At first, I didn't understand why, but eventually, I came to realize that they had truly done their best to support me in all of my previous academic endeavors. Simply put, they just weren't able to afford to do more. In my heart of hearts, I realized that that my parents had done all that they could do and had been the very best parents that anyone could have ever expected or hoped for, so now it was up to me to build on their initial efforts. I then made the decision that I would realize my dream to enter the college of my choice, just a little later on. I knew I had to work a job and that I had to trust that my dreams would come true.

Another reason I chose to go to a community college was that it was much more affordable for me to cover tuition. Because I would be working and commuting, this would now give me the opportunity to save money, so that I would be able to take advantage of a "pay as you go" plan. The final reason was that being in community college allowed me to focus on getting good grades, which was critical to transferring to another 4-year college or university. Although I had pretty much been a straight-A student in my elementary years, I lost some critical focus in high school. Therefore, when the time came, I didn't seek out scholarships. At that point, I believed that I didn't qualify for them. One other thing that I was determined to make sure was that I wouldn't go into debt. So because of the work/life and financial balance, I chose my course load based on what I could handle and what I could afford. I was actually the first, and still am the only person, in my immediate family to attend college and finish a college degree. I had no blueprint in my family from any immediate and extended family members because no one had ever completed this level of education.

Eventually, there were times where I had to work only and take time from classes to pay off bills in order to go back to school. I will never forget the crazy work hours, the many cold days at the bus stop, and finagling bus schedules that sometimes took having a 2-hour lead time on a bus that would normally be a 20-minute car ride. So the journey took a little over 2 years before I was finally able to apply to and be accepted to the 4-year university that I had dreamed of attending. After finally working so hard to "get there," midway in the semester of my junior year, a routine doctor's visit determined that I needed surgery. I could not wait according to my physician. He said I needed the surgery immediately. So that news completely threw me for a loop.

Now, I was weighted down with the fear of the unknown and the thought of interrupting my perfect plan. Should I at least try to get through this semester and risk my health? Or, should I just do what the doctor was recommending? The first thing I did was to get a second opinion from another physician. After it was confirmed that this procedure was a must and in my best interest now versus later, I chose my health over everything else. What good would I be at anything with this now plaguing my mind?

To prepare, I called all of my professors and asked them for an extension of time to complete my courses. I had to somehow retain the investment I had already made in the process. All but one of my professors was willing to work with me, which was his complete prerogative. His course was the only one I had to withdraw from, while the others allowed me as much time as I would need through the summer to complete their work.

Life is never easy. Life is unpredictable. Whether it's a personal illness or that of a loved one, dealing with a death or deaths, a financial crisis . . . you name it, there is minimal control or sometimes *no* control over when and how these circumstances "show up" in our lives. But there is one thing guaranteed: Things *are* going to show up.

Fortunately, I recovered from the surgery, but now had to

formulate a new plan to finish school. Six years of perseverance and determination to make this all happen versus the original plan of 4 consecutive years. Living through these circumstances and countless others, I realize there must be an overall deep love and passion with a relentless drive to pursue a dream, calling, or purpose. I would be absolutely remiss if I did not state that our own strength will be able to get us only so far.

It also takes doing (your part), believing, and understanding because you will face obstacles along your journey. Make up your mind that you will not let these things stop you; it is essential to your future success.

> *"Be Ready to Pay the Price to Make Your Dream Come True..."*
>
> —Author Unknown

Foundation Is the Key

My parents owned many very traditional and conservative views on who had what role of responsibility in the home just as many men and women still do. They truly "believed" that the husband was "supposed" to take care of "his" wife and "his" children. And the wife was supposed to bear the responsibility of caring for the home needs of the household. Amazingly enough, my dad actually believed that we belonged to him. He was very protective of his family on all fronts. He not only talked the talk, but he walked the walk with his actions. Same as my mom. I'm so thankful that I was raised by two very hardworking, committed adults who both willingly chose to unite, start, and actively support a family at a very young age at a time in life when this was viewed as proper and right in our society.

My parents were married at the tender age of 23 years old, and although that is definitely young on most accounts, I clearly recall their level of commitment to our family, even as a child. They were willing to give up so many of their personal ambitions to make sacrifices to meet their obligations as a couple and as parents to three growing children. My father and mother are the hardest working man and woman that I've ever known. They put in countless hours upon hours at their jobs and in the home, which equates to very long workdays for both of them. Although their work was laborious in nature, they both loved working within the framework of their respective roles, Dad's at his plant as a professional with sheet metal, and Mom's as homemaker extraordinaire, being an at-home mom and what I would also like to term as "other."

My mom, as she saw the need, would have stints of employment in the nursing industry, her second passion to her family. She usually did this to help bring in extra funds to support the family as needed. My parents had challenging work schedules because Dad worked the second shift and Mom took the very early shift or the third shift so that there was overlap and we could be with one of them at all times. My dad's demanding work schedule put Mom in the primary caregiver position, and meant she spent more time with us than he did.

During this time period in our society, society looked proudly to see a mother staying home to raise children. Back then, parents had distinctly different expectations of the roles that each parent would play in how the children should be raised and in the upkeep of the household. My mother was very traditional for the times. She would cook all the meals, take care of the chores in the home, and took great care of us while my father worked.

Although we were children and had the freedom to act as such, my mom kept things super organized in our home and in our lives. She had a day to go grocery shopping. Had a day to wash the clothes at the Laundromat. Also had a day to clean up our home. You noticed I said *home*. Although we did not own a house, per se, we were not deprived at all of having a home. Once, a stranger visited and asked my mom, "Is this apartment attached to this building, ma'am? You can literally eat off the floors, it's so clean in here." What a testament to a wonderful way of being raised.

My brothers and I weren't allowed to spend nights away often or with just anyone. We had to be accountable of our whereabouts at all times. I respect the decisions they made, especially now in the age where so many don't have that. The actions of my parents as a father/ husband and mother/wife are forever sealed in my mind. You probably didn't agree with each and every one of your parents' methods; however, I choose to focus on the underlying point that there was a very high level of commitment to family that I truly don't witness a lot of personally today. With that said, these behaviors are what laid a firm foundation of who I am and how I live my life now. And having come from this type of background, it has still taken me many years to own the very fact that how far I go really has little to do with everyone else. It mostly has to do with me and the choices that I choose to make.

Our willingness to make the necessary sacrifices is the key component of it all. I am a real believer in *what you sow is you are sure to reap*. Some like to use another term, *what goes around comes around*. Same idea no matter the lens you choose. This causes me to believe that what level I give of myself, that is the level that I should expect even a greater rate of return than I actually gave out. In the financial world, it's known as the "ROI," or return on investment.

In many cases, it's easy to want to shrug away the responsibility as to why something has not happened or is not happening in our lives, then on to the next thing. Instead, people tend to cite the lack of support from family and friends, the community, our teachers, our circumstances, the neighborhood we grew up in, the cat, and even the dog. It takes a certain level of maturity to begin to take responsibility for your own actions and YOUR life. The key starts with "you" looking inside of "you."

As an adult, I have learned that maturity and age are not always equal partners. In other words, the number of years behind the life does not equate to being a mature individual. These factors can literally be on different ends of the spectrum. Many people don't want to "grow up" in certain areas of their lives. Who has ever seen a grandma wear an outfit that was more suitable for her teenage granddaughter? Grandma's hair, makeup, and most of all, her mind-set, were off-kilter.

You can be yourself, and in the process, take some care in who "self" is and how will that "self" propel you to your purpose.

Never dumb down your individual blueprint on the world . . .

Nowadays, many people are getting "tatted," a short name for tattooed, but fail to think of how this action will come across in certain professional situations later on. How many times have you seen the show where people have gotten a lover's name or any massive amount of tattoos on their body and now have regrets and want to alter their choices? In life, that is what has to be considered when it comes to our brand. How will my actions impact or alter my brand? Realize that this is "our world," but we're not the only ones who live in it. There are laws, there are expectations, and there are standards of living.

The same goes for the older man who doesn't necessarily come across as acting his age. Some of these men are seen with baseball caps turned backward, hoodies, sagging jeans, and gym shoes. It's not completely the attire; there's yelling, "This is just not right . . ." and other mannerisms. Some men in certain age groups have been known to allegedly be labeled as being in a "midlife crisis" when certain behaviors tend to arise. The entire concept behind being in a midlife crisis is the fact that people are in some denial of getting older, and all that comes with aging. Like not having enough stamina, developing wrinkles, losing hair, etc.

Whether it is streaming processes or the updating of technology, there is no room left for the antiquated (a nonupdated way of doing something). I would have used the word "old," but nowadays, that may not be the best possible descriptor. Why is that? Old isn't really old.

And that is okay, but I must admit, in all honesty, I absolutely do not care for the term "getting old." Now to be the one on the outside looking in, you may never know this about me. That's why sharing who we are when warranted is so important.

There was a time where no matter who asked me to do something for them, I didn't have the courage to say "no." For example, something as simple as my mom calling me while I'm at work. I'm tired, maybe even having a rough day, and I just don't want to do it, but I'll say "yes." Now, because I already, deep down, didn't want to, now I'm in the store not in the best mood, and, of course, everything wrong is amplified. The item I want is out of stock, it's taking an exceptionally long time, the noncustomer service-oriented worker, who, of course, is supposed to understand that I've had a difficult day, didn't want to be here in the first place and she can't read my mind. Now I'm frustrated with the situation, and my mom is frustrated with me. All I had to do is simply say, "no," and not wonder if my mom would still love me or not. I had to learn that love is not always a self-sacrifice, and it's quite okay to have the people that love you not always like the choices you make if you know that is the right choice for you at the time.

Everything action or nonaction affects our life; that's just the way it's set up. Now, I can put myself out there as an example. I believe most people have a comfort food that it's best to stay away from. Mine are chocolate and pizza. I just can't stop eating them once they're in arm's reach. Well, I know that's not good, so I have to monitor how often and what quantity I consume. There's nothing distinctly wrong with chocolate or pizza in and of themselves. What's wrong is my response to eating these foods. No one's holding me hostage and forcing either one in my mouth, so I do have some control over the situation . . . right?

No one in my family had ever done it before. I had nothing to base this fact on other than in my inner knowing and faith to believe. I knew some way, somehow, that it would happen.

My parents were working-class citizens that lived in the inner city of Chicago, on the "west side" which is nicknamed by some as the "best side." But I paid our location no mind. I didn't notice the poverty and other struggling families in the building and neighborhood. I was so proud of my family and all that it stood for. What did I know to let me think otherwise? I had a roof over my head. I never went to bed hungry at night, and back in the 1970s in my world, having these basic amenities meant that everything was all right. I ignored the facts; the things around me, but I chose to listen to the truth (also defined as my belief). The fact that Momma and Daddy, at that time, although great people, were living from paycheck to paycheck in their one-bedroom apartment. I hadn't noticed.

This was the beginning of a self-fulfilling journey, and just like many of you, there is something that you know you want to do, but sometimes you just can't figure out all of the pieces and steps that it will take to help get you there. It must be realized by as individuals the intentionality and clarity of how living life in its basic structure has taught us as people how much of an importance one should commit to as it relates to care of himself (themselves). Outwardly, when it comes to something as basic as personal hygiene for things such as being clean and well-groomed and being dressed in appropriate attire for the occasion, these items are, in some cases, a deal breaker for a date, the close of a business transaction, that next speaking opportunity—you name it.

> *There are two sides to self-branding; how you see yourself first, and then how you feel you are being perceived by others.*

If you didn't put your makeup on or just "threw" on any old something to wear (not ironed, not even necessarily matching), that is a direct reflection of you. Go figure. Wouldn't *this* be the day that you run into that someone that you now wished could have seen you in a different light? If you could redo it, you would have been a bit more together . . . a bit more polished. This has happened to me on more than one occasion, and I had the same afterthought. *Man, I should not have put that hat on my head, and why didn't I have on some makeup, at least some lip gloss? Jeez.*

What has developed into habits in the small sense of living will directly impact what will develop bigger later on. Our belief system is important to what we **can** accomplish in our lives. This is the instance that you *should* "sweat the small stuff." No, this is not a free ticket to be overly self-indulgent and overdose into a selfish, self-centered type. I don't condone vain actions that are inconsiderate of the next person or persons. I define it as showing you care about you, and there is nothing wrong with that mind-set. Your mind-set defines your belief system (belief system = mind-set).

If the doctor is really convinced of your need to have surgery, he or she, in most instances, willingly encourages you to seek a second opinion, or possibly even a third or fourth, depending on the severity of the illness. A caring doctor, in my opinion, is sensitive to the emotional surges within his/her patient and realizes the anxiety one may face on all fronts when dealing with matters that severely affect health. First, there is the fear of the unknown. Just the thought of having surgery can make anyone nervous and can be true agony, even with loved ones supporting you along in the process. Clearly, walking into the operating room without reviewing a patient's medical history, extending time the patient and their loved ones to expend all options in the scenario, along with the possible outcome (both good and bad have to be a vital part of the "preparation" process).

Although support systems may be in place, when you are being rolled into an operating room and are about to go under anesthesia, your life can begin "flashing before your eyes." Going under the lights is quite overwhelming and intimidating, based on the potential risks involved. A room full of experimental minds and shiny utensils leaves you in a completely vulnerable state of mind. This is the point where you are opening up yourself to a process that you are hopeful will improve your condition.

The process for surgery has absolutely nothing to do with that other aspect: recovery. Recovery represents the *time* and *process* it takes to heal. That could be bed rest, therapy, or just following the doctor's orders.

This is an example of the steps that my doctor took, or any ethically sound medical professional would take, to care for his patient in order to provide a proper diagnosis of your condition. In the same approach, there are certain skills that can lead to a healthy mind-set when considering your brand. What you do to help prepare yourself to be your best brand is part of your brand health.

This conceptualization also steers me to think of individuals I'd met over the years that have shared their military experiences in boot camp, also known as "basic training." I've had been told that this opportunity warrants consistent expectations for the newbies, which is a determinant if they will last the required duration of the process or ultimately give in to the pressures and extreme stimuli that they're bombarded with. This is the time where new habits were being formed. In both cases, both of the people I knew were just starting their adult lives, which meant that fears of the future for certain were at the top of their thinking.

Additionally, being pulled out of their normal comfort zones, having to relocate to a different state and being surrounded by complete strangers, who are determining who you trust, contributes to being a risk taker. Finally, starting a brand-new life in a highly disciplined setting brings its own set of challenges.

First, they were told when to go to bed and also when they had to rise; then, they were expected to do whatever they were told. Keep in mind these factors took no consideration of who the night owls or early birds were. Everyone simply had to adjust and do it without complaints or visible resistance. The expectation was to report to the area and be assessed for the basics (i.e., ironed clothing, straight posture, weaponry, submissive attitude, etc.).

This type of uncanny environment required a mind-set of flexibility which was just as important to have, while maintaining a good attitude/disposition (inward focus) to be successful. No one wants to deal with negative people, especially those who are trying to head in a positive direction with their life. This is only a microsnapshot of the life of a budding soldier. In the end, making it through this process was the beginning of their hopes, aspirations, and dreams. The great takeaway here is that one must be willing to put in the work to be set up for success.

When you see someone who takes care of their basics, and they step it up to be their best and not just be mediocre, it is clearly evident how they present themselves in everything they do. This is where we can take note of the term *quality over quantity*. For example, I'd rather experience quality relationships and experiences any day over less meaningful or empty experiences.

The concept of branding must be woven into all areas of our lives in a holistic manner; from personal, to professional, and to spiritual perspectives.

When I was informed of the circumstances surrounding my condition, at that time, I had to stop my coursework during my second semester at the university I had dreamed of attending. My plans and my timetable went right out the window.

It's the Little Things

Your motivation typically is what drives your heart, and the matter of the heart spills over into how you choose to lead life as an individual. This is not to say that you are walking around striving to be some perfect person, but what it does mean is that you are striving to do what is right and to be a person of excellence. There's also a scripture that states a little leaven leavens the whole lump. Another way that has been said is that one rotten apple can spoil the whole bunch. For example, after assembling what is thought to be a dream team, all of a sudden, there are red flags of one person showing resistance in a derogatory way. This can cause greater issues of concern later down the road.

Your House in Order (Figuratively and Literally)

As hard as it is to face a poor decision you made or a bill you can't pay, just deal with it. I've heard people say that the "good guys" or "good people" finish last. I tend to disagree with that based on what I have observed in my years here on earth. In other words, as you do the good things, good things will come back to you.

> *When you are promoting your brand, one thing I truly believe is that people have to trust that you are "believable." If I can't believe in you, your credibility, your dependability, how can I trust you and have confidence in you?*

It is so important that you are able to gain and keep trust in your relationships. Although I don't believe there are perfect people, I do believe that part of success is maintaining our integrity. I can distinctly recall several instances when I had the opportunity to volunteer in various ministry departments in my church of 20 years. The obvious part is 20 years of your life spent anywhere, giving of your time, talent, and resources, you should believe in the mission and vision.

In the course of serving at my church, I worked closely with various leaders. The reality is, no matter if it's a church, a charity, a corporation, working with and among different personalities, in most instances, requires a great deal of humility and willingness to be flexible. The one thing I was never willing to compromise was my integrity in any situation—especially one that was in the household of faith.

My positions meant I had multiple and overlapping roles, but they all reported to the pastor of the church. Well, I'm sure you can imagine leaders do not all see eye to eye and do not necessarily get along. So with that said, I had to see our leader navigate through all types of dilemmas, whether ministering to parishioners, counseling couples, intervening in family disputes, you name it. The greatest point is that a pastor, as any other manager, is appointed to do a job. In all of my pastor's mistakes, the one quality that helped me believe and continue believing in the work was his willingness to accept responsibility. When the need arose, he would apologize and strive to move forward in fairness and truth. I know that might not mean much to many, or seem important to some, but that was a big deal to me.

Self-Development, Three as: Attitude, Aptitude & Appearance

I'm a firm believer in the concept that people must never stop being open to learning. The term in education known as being a "lifelong learner" lets us know that there is always room for more knowledge, more growth, and more development. As such, you must think seriously what are you doing to hone your brand? In other words, how are you choosing to enhance who you are, which simply means, making you better. Depending on your chosen profession or industry, the requirements for continual learning and excelling may vary. But the goal is the same. Seek to be a better you. In your craft and in your life.

Preparation Is a Mind-set

A vision is being able to see your dream *before* it is realized. A vision is being able to "imagine." I'm a firm believer that you must see it, and then you must "see it." You must see or be able to visualize the way you want to see yourself in your head, and you must be able to see it in your heart, if that makes sense. Being the first to believe that what you want to achieve can happen once is indeed a game changer. This is where the term *mind-set* comes from. The very first time I heard this terminology used in context, I had no clue what it meant. I eventually figured it out. The definition is simple: *it's how you think.*

> *So many times, we are the first destroyers of what we would positively believe we are able to accomplish in our lives.*

Self-sabotaging. How many times can you recall setting out to try or do something and thoughts arose, defeating your purpose before you even got a chance to get started? Why is that? What is that thing which allows others to have the inner strength to still move forward?

You have to believe you can before anyone else will believe you can.

> *"Dress for the job you want, and not just for the job that you have."*
>
> —UNKNOWN

Also, don't try to do so many things, but just focus on one. That can be a hard thing if you're the type of person who, like myself, likes a variety of things and who has been blessed with a diverse group of talents.

I've shared with students time and time again, any skill you learn in life is never wasted. It's up to you to identify what are deemed as "transferable skills." Transferable skills are ones that you will use in life. Communication is an example and a transferable skill. No matter the chosen profession, this skill is critical. Listening is another example of a much-needed skill.

Whether you aspire to be a surgeon or a singer, both require much preparation prior to the "performance." In the example of the medical profession, it's up to the doctor to do his/her research on the patient's medical condition and history prior to any surgical procedure. They can't just show up wearing scrubs and have scalpel in hand, saying, "All right, what do we got here?"

Of course, in the example of emergency room doctors, there is an entirely different dynamic. I am referring to what may be the traditional scope how you identify due to medical attention that you have a need for intervention and how you proceed down the path to better your health. I know a little bit about how this goes, having endured two instances of surgeries in my lifetime. The first was a semiemergency, as my doctor basically said you need to do it now or suffer these potential consequences. The other was much different as I identified my condition, sought treatment options over a number of months, and planned to go through with the procedure that was not life-threatening, however, potentially, life-altering.

Image Is Everything: Yay or Nay?

Is image everything? The answer is unequivocally yes. Image IS everything. I know I've touched a little bit on the topic of physical appearance, but I can't emphasize this point enough. Do you remember the slogan, *what you see is what you get?* I think appearance plays a huge role and affects many factors of our lives. Image is directly tied to appearance, and how we convey this as an individual or organization does greatly impact our brand. This aspect defined, however, goes a lot deeper than merely "just" how you look. Image allows the cognitive or mental picture of one to go on to a greater dimension and scope, lending to how someone or something is ultimately perceived and presented in your mind. This can be based on fact or by other factors, which, in some cases, are linked to the opinions of others. Whenever entertaining the opinions of others, this concept can be experienced in a much-broader scope. For example, some points of perceptions have been formulated on what you were taught or exposed to in your formative years of development. These perceptions can influence different aspects of our life and the opinions we form as a result.

Usually, there is a central core of influencers that participate in the development of this in your life—parents, siblings, teachers, mentors, etc.

Let's say that you've heard the term "all men are dogs," which is based on someone else's experience. When you're dating and things don't necessarily work in your favor in the relationship, now you'll begin to form an opinion based on your experience combined with that statement. From that point on, you'll possibly connect someone else's experience to your life or opinion slate.

Another example could be, let's say you're hosting a meeting with new potential business partners and the one person who shows up late is a person of color, and immediately you assume they are on "CP" time. For anyone who needs further clarification, when someone says you're on "CP" time, they're saying you are, or you're going to be, late. There is nothing positive about its connotation. On another level, it can actually be offensive as "CP" is the acronym for "colored people," which further implies that colored people are always late. People have a time management problem in every ethnic background, yet, no one ever says "CP" (white people) or "LP" (Latino people) time.

Practice behaviors that represent your goals and always put you in a positive light. The reality of the "CP" example above is that the individual who arrived late may have simply run into some horrific accident that held up traffic, or maybe the individual simply got lost because they had never been to this meeting location before. Whatever the case may be, to instantly form a negative opinion about any situation without having the details is definitely unwise. Now, for those who consistently are late, your opinion may be justified.

There is a level of accountability that exists when you involve others in the equation. Communication is one of the greatest tools **we** will ever possess to get the desired message out about our brand. My general practice when I am expected to be at a place by a certain time is to always understand what time it is in relation to the time I committed to be there. If I can gauge approximately 15 to 20 minutes prior that there is a slight possibility that I will not make it on time, as a courtesy, I call and identify my location. Having people wait on you with no understanding of your whereabouts is a brand travesty. It's basically rude and disrespectful in some circles of life. Don't let a behavior or stereotype define you.

This is the age where there are so many possible ways to communicate, it leaves us with very few excuses—phone, text, e-mail, Skype. Then there are timers, alarms, and Global Positioning Systems (GPS) in our vehicles (and on our smartphones). From my view, all of the necessary potential tools are in place to help us be successful, organized, and ready for whatever comes our way. Most of all, the most important human resource that will set the tone for our image and our brand is *us*.

12

BUILDING A BRAND: PASSION & PURPOSE

I recently attended an event where one of the speaker's topics was *"Purpose, Passion & Goals."* The one part of the presentation that stood out the most was when the questions were posed to the audience: *"Do you know your purpose in life, why are you here?"* I saw mature (30-plus years) adults who did not raise their hands. Some may tend to think, if you don't know why you're here by age 30-plus, then you have made yourself vulnerable to whatever, whenever, however.

A few weeks back, I struck up a conversation with the clerk at the doctor's office. She was still trying to "figure out" her calling in life. Well, she had indicated prior to that comment that she had a daughter in college and had been married over 20 years. I was internally floored with concern for her.

Everyone is here for a specific purpose, and when it's understood what that is, then and only then will there be a "true" contentment. I'm not saying you will know the specifics of how you will get there, but you should at least know the direction in which you're going, and get on your way. I may not be familiar with all the highway routes that will get me to Texas, but I know that it is south of Illinois. If I do my research, I can get help and a better understanding of how to get there via several means: maps, MapQuest, talking to people who have been there, etc.

So here are a few pointers to help get you there:

1. Seek direction . . .
   First and foremost, I believe in the "power of praying" for guidance. Now that's me (but do you). In addition to prayer, I believe one way to avoid a ton of mistakes is listening to good counsel. Whether a family member, a trusted mentor, even a professional, do what you have to do to get where you need to go.

2. Pursue what you're passionate about . . .
   Find ways to do what you love, even if you don't get paid at the onset. Having passion is the key to your success. You will rarely see people do well at something they have limited interest or passion in. What is passion? It's that burning desire to succeed. Passion is the thing that brings you complete satisfaction and joy.

3. Don't stop until you see progress, no matter how small . . .
   You will then begin to know when you're on that right track for your life.

Eric Bassett is the owner of EB30X and one of my Facebook friends. He lives and breathes fitness. He is the forerunner and model of someone who's in great spirits and great shape. Eric is now producing production clips of trainings, as well as various events. He is going far because he is, above all, fueling his dream with something that can only come from within. He clearly loves what he's doing.

Passion is a compelling desire for something. Passion is a feeling of enthusiasm or excitement for something or about doing something. So what are *you* passionate about? You can't fake passion, nor can you duplicate it. So my charge to you . . . Conduct a true inventory and reflective exercise on where your passions lie. I've noticed that frequently, many tend to put their passions on the back burner, but I hope this book will encourage you to pursue that which is important to you. Life is short, so focus on the areas in your life that bring you the most joy. Sometimes, time is wasted on things that are not developing skills or things that don't hold our interests. Do your passion and do it now!

Brand Innovation

Can you recall ever seeing something that seemed "way out there" or "before our time"? I attended a conference in recent years called *Tech Talk* where nearly one hundred vendors set up with their gadgets and demos. I ran into a colleague wearing a pair of Google eyeglasses, officially referred to as "Google Glass." Well, they are not just your typical eyeglasses; they're like wearing a computer with frames on your face with an optical lens. "*Google Glass displays information through what is similar to a smartphone with a hands-free format,*"—*Wikipedia*. My colleague was chosen among a selected few to be a tester for this newly launched product. Basically, she had an edge over everyone at the conference because she was the one who really stood out with her product literally on her face. I barely was able to say hello because different attendees were stopping her to ask questions about this "unique" piece of work she was displaying.

One strategy I've heard a bit about lately that ensures the best use of time is to make appointments with yourself, which means you will need a planner. The suggestion is to actually pencil in time with you. Just like you make doctor appointments or any other type, add what you need to accomplish to your personal calendar and don't break appointments with yourself.

Distraction Our #1 Hindrance

There's absolutely nothing wrong with Ma-and-Pa type shops because these are the backbones of communities and have brilliant visionaries at the helm. However, depending on what your vision is for yourself, you have to think chain stores, you have to think world-wide. How far do you want to go?

There is an old saying, you only get out what you put in. I'm the type who's just never been quite satisfied with only staying on my own block . . . I want more. I've also heard opportunity doesn't come knocking at your door, opportunity awaits you, and you must not sell yourself short. Avail yourself to new opportunities. Don't continue to settle for just the same ol' thing.

I recall a former friend who had an aunt who stated she would never leave her block. Other than for mere errands, this was her home for life. She actually believed that this was it for her. I also remember having had a couple of neighbors who vowed the home they were in would be their final home, and one who literally had anxiety attacks if she even considered walking off our block.

Even more so in today's society, you have to literally fight for your time. It takes time to get things done. From the basics of keeping a clean home to outside chores, sometimes, it has taken me a half day just to thoroughly clean the kitchen. I mean the dishes, washing cabinets, organizing food, cleaning out the refrigerator, and mopping the floor. It can be a BIG project. Even preparing a tasty meal takes time. I love to cook for others, but it's work. That's why this generation is nicknamed the microwave generation because they have a "give it to me now" attitude. But I am in the fight of my life, and that fight is for time. Let's reclaim our lives and learn to prioritize things in a healthy, balanced way.

I believe in working hard and doing a quality job for any organization, but there has to be a balance, and that's what seems to be missing. Especially when there is a spouse and children and possibly other commitments like taking care of elderly parents, or more so nowadays, raising grandchildren.

If we do not balance ourselves properly, we may tend to never feel full satisfaction, even after so many accomplishments.

Take my writing as an example. To get through this process, I've had to do a number of different things. I've given myself calendar dates for the completion of so many pages per day. I've had to break it down even further in order to actually give myself a particular number of hours to devote to writing. It has even forced me to set a goal to write so many words per day. You may not be able to nail your niche the first time, so some things are trial and error until you figure out what works.

Author, speaker, and life coach, Valorie Burton has stated, "*Direct your thoughts and energy toward the goals you want to accomplish.*"

13

DON'T BE AFRAID TO BE DIFFERENT . . .

Many of my greatest growing up pains were experienced in my younger years when I believed I had the power to convince those who I did not connect with that I wasn't any different than they. That was never a job I should have taken on. In healthy relationships, the acceptance of who you are should be a natural thing.

When you start to display who you are to people, you are now welcoming them to your brand. Be mindful and brace yourself to understand that they have a choice of accepting or rejecting you. And it's completely okay to for them to make whatever choice that they choose. Healthy relationships are right relationships. When you start to think that maybe something is wrong with you being you in the truest sense of who you are, that is the day you will start to limit your brand reach. Don't allow yourself to start having all types of thoughts and reactions that can distort reality. Always remember you don't fit in anywhere but where you belong. Get rid of the "stinking thinking."

You Are a Custom Design

The movie *Inside Man* with lead actors Clive Owen, Academy Award Winners Denzel Washington and Jodie Foster, along with a premier cast, forges a plot where a mastermind plans to execute a major bank heist in Manhattan, New York, over a 24-hour period. In the movie's ending, which wasn't traditional by any means, he got away with it.

Thou Shall Prosper . . .

Prosperity is one of the most sought after things today. Everywhere in mainstream media are programs on how you can succeed in this, with training on how to accomplish that. There's a three-step, five-step, 10-step, and 12-step . . . But I'm going to let you in on the one-step program as it has been told to those who want to get straight to the heart of the matter. One must have his or her priorities set in the right order to get what he or she thinks they deserve. Many people desire the tangibles, such as a new home, a fancy car, or a good job. Sometimes the intangibles are also pursued: a strategy, a solution, a healing, and a discipline in a particular area of our life. More than anything else, your soul will prosper best knowing your purpose on earth. So, advance and be fulfilled and pursue what you need to. When you're doing exactly what you were created to do right, everything will align right up just for you!

14

I'M REBRANDING: A CAREER GAME CHANGER

Many individuals are suffering from unemployment or underemployment. Unemployment is the state of wanting a job, or where you are actively seeking one out, or where you are in the stage of waiting to be hired. Underemployment, on the other hand, is when you may be overqualified for the position that you currently hold. Additionally, you also may not be receiving a full benefits package (i.e., healthcare options, savings match, vacation days, etc.) that meets previous standards of which you attained and/or you are simply being underpaid on all accounts based on work experience, prior pay, and benefits. Underpayment can also be based on what the going rate of pay is for the job and compared to what you were offered and accepted. Many people are taking on this type of work based on the theory that "something is better than nothing." Maybe you've been out there on the job hunt for quite some time, and there just aren't enough bites. Sometimes these types of opportunities are often accepted because you simply need to work.

Many difficult decisions must be made when you are put in a position of needing to work to survive. We may never know what circumstances may befall us, and some have just resolved themselves that they simply must accept this work situation just to "keep it moving." This mind-set requires one to develop a level of flexibility in thinking. One of the greatest career lessons that could ever be learned is the ability to move with change. There are certain types of change welcomed wholeheartedly, and others, not so much.

Some forms of change are initiated, and others are inflicted upon us. For those initiated forms of change, sometimes coming to terms that something or a "state of existence in a matter of being" must be done differently in our manner of affairs. It could be a correction in our behavior. Perhaps you will work on actually being a better listener. How can you show active listening? By giving someone eye contact or not multitasking while they are speaking. These are little things, however, it means a lot to that person with whom you are engaging. Show someone that you've heard them and take note of their concerns. Work to make the necessary adjustments in your communication skills.

Whether working for a company, organization, or for yourself as an entrepreneur, maintain an attitude of flexibility and an openness for change. Our world is in constant invent mode. Somewhere, someone is stowed away working on the next best thing in fashion, music, technology, education, film, you name it. And then upon its completion and launch into the world, there is enjoyment of those creative works for a season or even for a lifetime. Then the cycle repeats itself. When I think of all this, my head is left spinning.

American society is generally very fast paced, and the wait is not always that long for anything. Some may term it the "microwave" mentality. We want it sooner than later and bigger than ever, and, yes, we actually expect a bigger bang for our buck. It's astounding how when you study those who have achieved significant accomplishments, sometimes they are not looking to just outdo their competitors, they are looking to outdo themselves.

Take Apple Inc., a phenomena created by the late cofounder, chairman, and CEO, Steve Paul Jobs. According to research, he brought Apple Inc. back from bankruptcy to profitability in 1998, and stayed on track to what has been described as one of the "greatest turnarounds in business history." There is more to the story that occurred prior to the year 1998, but this aspect is clearly a great example of Mr. Job's expertise to reinvent himself, and the company was regarded, while he was at its helm, as the premier strategist inventor, marketer, and entrepreneur. One would probably agree that Steve Jobs was indeed a pioneer and one who knew how to effectively embrace change. The word *embrace* is key to our success when in this process.

Keep a Positive, Adaptable Brand

No one wants to be around a person who is carrying a critical spirit. Even Bible scriptures warn us about "murmuring and complaining." Often, when you feel you've been dealt a poor hand, so to speak, it becomes easier to fall in this mode or mind-set. However, it's important to maintain the frame of mind that change is inevitable, whether we're ready for it or not. So when the change comes, be willing to reinvent and redo in order to adapt.

Rebranding: The Chef Jeff Story

Jeff Henderson's story is an urban fairy-tale depiction of how an individual went from "rags to riches" and proved that it is neither impossible nor ever too late to make the proper changes in your life. Chef Jeff went from being a troubled youth to a self-made success. He was raised by his grandparents and his mother on the volatile streets of Central Los Angeles. After a near-death experience as a teenager due to being involved in gang activity, he moved away to the Southern California city of San Diego. There, he got caught selling narcotics, which landed him in prison for 10 years.

I suspect the person who is incarcerated has so much time to think and reflect while in that circumstance. And I believe many have the "I wish I would have or could have" syndrome.

While serving his prison term, Jeff chose to begin the process to turn his life around. There, he was mentored by a fellow inmate as a cook in the prison kitchen. Jeff developed his passion for cooking, which led to the dream of becoming an executive chef one day. Upon his release, one of his strategies for moving forward was him making some immediate changes in his appearance. He took the earring out and covered the hole with makeup. He shaved off his beard and mustache and learned all about dressing "the part." From there, he began moving forward to pursue his dream.

Jeff has gone on to become the first African American chef in several major Las Vegas hotels, eventually landing his dream job of executive chef at several well-known Las Vegas hotels. Jeff has written his own story in the *New York Times* best-selling book, *Cooked*. Now, Jeff is a thriving award-winning chef, best-selling author, and popular public speaker (just to name a few of his accolades), and an inspiration to so many others. Branding himself then and now is part of the story of Jeff Henderson. Having realized that if he wanted to become the person in that dream, he had to do something different. No matter what others may say or think, I guarantee you a great portion of how Jeff was perceived made a difference in him being chosen for the positions he went on to garner in his career as a chef. Jeff first had to believe in the possibility that he could have those positions.

The whole concept of doing what it takes to change your reality requires a certain type of approach, or conditioning, first, starting with the way you think. As a man thinks, so he is. You will become what you expect to become.

What was it that propelled Jeff to actually believe that he could go from the "prison to the palace"? This reminds me of Joseph in the Bible. Not exactly alike, but the inspiration of it all is that both went on to do great things. So what else did Jeff and Joseph have? Confidence. Jeff had no "formal" training in this role, but he believed that he could secure it if he put his mind to it. He did not know all of the details of how, but I know he internalized a vision (saw what could be) of what he believed was possible.

It's about the Business (Entrepreneur Edition)

A dynamic individual named Shirley W. showed me the ropes and how to always maintain a certain positive posture (attitude) with the customers. After my training period in the lobby, also the location where the banking executives worked, at any given time, I could be approached by almost anyone. There were times when the president or managers would come over and strike up a conversation or bring a very important transaction to process for a new wealthy client. There were other instances when the locals, who visited almost every single day, stopped in to bring their deposits.

A longtime resident, probably a seasoned community member, came in with all the community updates. I like the word *updates* versus, *gossip*. The bank where I worked was the type of organization that tellers could cash the payroll checks of local warehouse workers, the city's law enforcement officers, or that of a millionaire. They were all important, and they all needed to be treated with the same respect.

Treating all people the same should be a general practice or mindset of any business or organization. We are currently in a crisis right now because some who have been appointed to *serve and protect* are not giving fair and equal treatment to all. But the truth of the matter is, there is no excuse to ever condone poor and unethical treatment of anyone.

You have both internal and external key stakeholders to your organization.

The Best Position to Take Is that EVERYONE Is a Customer

When I moved from business to the education sector, I did not abandon this concept. My clients went from business owners to students, parents, fellow colleagues, community members, and other key constituents, just to name a few.

How you manage customer relationships will always determine if the message of your brand will remain effective.

Imagine political figures. They tend to campaign for the purpose of winning you over. This is the time they will tell you what they can do, what they commit to do, and in most cases, how they are going to do it. This causes you to "buy into" the brand message of one opponent over the other. Then there's the moment of truth. If your candidate wins and when the appointment comes, now your standards for what will be accomplished are set because of the "brand promise." If those expectations are not met, they are no longer seen in the same light. The brand image becomes tarnished. Living up to customer expectations that you've set are indeed a component of your brand's ability to stand the test of time. No brand would exist without its set group of customers.

Consistency Is the Key . . .

There's a social media frenzy. It's time to seize the moment. It's important to check the authenticity of those you're choosing to do business with. Three prep 101 examples. There should be an option for all potential customers to be able to speak to those providing a service. One of the up-and-coming ways to do this is through social media.

The way your brand is portrayed in today's media is important. Nowadays, if you are choosing the media route (it's practically impossible not to), you have opened yourself to a certain amount of vulnerability to the world of cyberspace that can be linked back to the world, and more specifically—*your* world.

Every sector has been touched with a form of technology advancement, whether a Web site, check-in system, e-mails, news articles, blogs, and your social media posts.

People are literally sabotaging themselves on so many levels. It's as if the social media forum has become a place to vent your innermost thoughts, and sometimes, that can be more dangerous than anything else imaginable.

One thing in this world that is inevitable is . . . *change*. Change is something that can't be stopped. Think about seasons. I've always lived in the part of the country where I've had the luxury of experiencing four seasons in the year: spring, summer, fall, and winter. Each one carries its own set of requirements as the way to live in them. The seasons for some affect their mental approach to the world. For example, some absolutely love spring, while others absolutely hate the winter months. I've met folks who absolutely adore snow and cold of winter because they did not grow up in a winter environment. I almost despise Chicago winters.

Growing up in winter personifies the Incredible Hulk aka "the Hulk," because that cold comes to the city where I live with a sort of vengeance.

Change is just like the seasons of our lives. Sometimes change is necessary. How can one expect to move forward if he or she is not willing to take the necessary steps? Albert Einstein said, *"Insanity: doing the same thing over and over again and expecting different results."* How can you expect anything different if you're not willing to *do* something different? That's just like vowing you're going to lose those extra 30 pounds, but you make no effort to change any of your eating, exercising, or sleeping habits. What do you expect as far as results, this being the case? It would be insane to expect a change in your condition if you do nothing to prepare yourself by making the necessary steps. The weight is not going to fall off by magic. Many people having struggled with being overweight sometimes just want to throw in the towel.

The general problem of obesity has skyrocketed in our country, especially among the youth. A national campaign to change this is at the top of the agenda for our first lady of the United States, Michelle Obama, called "Let's Move," which promotes healthier eating choices and exercise for children and their families. This movement has impacted the school system's approach to food and what's being served to students on a daily basis. It is also designed to spill over into the family life habits as well, coaching the parents on how to make better nutritional choices to present in the home.

Being overweight and obesity are certainly not just an issue for children, but for adults alike. I've found this to be one of the things that I am consistently addressing as an adult, even reflecting personally on those 30 pounds that I mentioned in my example. I have to remain conscientious all the time about my food choices, or I'll just eat whatever I want, whenever, and how much of whatever it is I want or crave. I was able to do this growing up because I was super skinny. As time has went on, my metabolism changed. That is not the behavior that will cause me to win this particular battle.

Something in me just refuses to settle for my body not being in its greatest possible health condition.

Ultimately, you are responsible to work your own goals and dreams if you want to see them become a reality. Sitting idly by will cause nothing to happen in your favor. *It's not by luck or by happenstance that goals are met, but life has to be lived on purpose.*

Being a human being is truly complex. We are intricately made, which reflects the brilliancy of the master of the universe. So now this complex creature is striving to find out the reason he's on the planet too.

Sometimes after much toiling and perseverance, we finally land our "dream" job, or as close to it that we can get. But then at the next quarterly budget meeting, it's announced that the company is downsizing or is going through a restructure also known as a "re-org." Now your fate has now fallen into the hands of someone else. That's the reality of the corporate industry, the politics of business transactions, and you're now back at square one in your career. If no one else buys into your dream, *you* must buy into your dream.

Or let's say you thought you were thriving and striving in your career, and all of a sudden, your boss walks in with the "surplus" conversation, and that there is going to be some company downsizing. However the news was communicated, you are now forced out of your position with no certain future. Will you become hostile and hateful and start badmouthing the organization based on where the chips have fallen? Or will you see the glass half full and use this as an opportunity to do some soul-searching and determine . . . Is this the best time to move to another part of the organization or to another similar organization, like a competitor? Or is this the time to make a major career change altogether? Whatever you choose to do in this type of situation, never lose sight of being a brand.

No one will ever take to heart your hopes and dreams like you. Your life has to be your priority and not someone else's option. If you are not satisfied with some aspect of your life, make the change to make it different.

Most everyone I know in the state of mind of not being fully fulfilled want to see results; they're ready for a change. I'm sure you can relate to having heard this resounding cry from many of those you come in contact with too. So now, let's veer away from focusing on other folks at this moment and let's turn the focus on to you. Where are you in life's crossroad of change or transition? Consider the term known as a "strategic inflection point." Envision in your mind a four-way intersection, which obviously presents four choices of direction. As you merge on to the intersection from your location, there are clearly other choices (three to be exact) that will lead to a different direction. You now have the choice to forge straight-ahead, staying on your current course of action, or you can choose another "course" or option. It's up to you to make the best possible choice that will impact you further down the road.

Don't expect a change if you're not willing to do what it takes to accomplish something new.

There was a dead heat in the Democratic Party between the now President Barack Obama and the former Secretary of State Hillary Rodham Clinton. The point made was no matter who I liked or disliked, change was coming, whether or not I "got on board," so to speak. A change was coming to the White House, irrespective of my support or lack thereof; change to the next administration was inevitable. So that would be the same for today. Whether one buckles down and really gets a vision for how to achieve the goal and dreams in our lives, life is going to keep on moving, and in some instances, pass some by. Life isn't concerned that you are a procrastinator; it's going to keep on moving. Life really has no opinion on your goals and dreams either way. It's really all up to you.

"Life is what you make it. Always has been, always will be."

—Eleanor Roosevelt

That next level to achieve your goals may include a career change, changing particular relationships, choosing to live a healthier lifestyle, having a baby with your spouse, moving to another state . . . You name it. But whatever you are contemplating, it's time to act on that which will begin to gear your life into your desired state. It's time to act on those dreams and make them a reality.

One of the greatest dream killers is procrastination, although there are others. I envision the dream killer of procrastination to be directly related to some other dream killers; you know, cousin fear, and let's not forget uncle time-robber, and how about aunt "I never complete anything."

Time is a commodity. Time cannot be regained when it has not been used to the fullest. There's no such thing as "banking" or "preserving" time. This leads to a very important point: There is no more time to remain stagnate or passive about our lives. Life is a special gift that must be treated as such.

The primary question to ask is . . . "What do I need to do to execute what I want in order to just even begin the steps to start seeing my dream realized?" Also, ask yourself, "What do I have right now (resources) that can get the ball rolling?" One popular mainstream slogan goes, "What's in your wallet?" I would rephrase this question, "What resources do you *already* have that can be allocated to your dream?" Get a pen and paper and start writing.

Where there is an overwhelming desire to finish what you've started, or, at least, to just get started: the 4 *P*s: Passion, Purpose, Possibilities, and Pace should play a part.

1. Passion
   You must have a deep interest and desire for the endeavor. So whether singer, writer, poet, entrepreneur, or preacher, there should be something driving you to go to the highest heights and deepest depths. Just know no one should be more convinced about fulfilling your dream than *you*.

2. Purpose
   Typically, what you have a passion for is your purpose. Your purpose is defined as the thing you're supposed to do

in life. Or what I would say is your raison d'êter or "reason for being."

3. Possibilities

   This is the point of deep dreaming. This is where you can plan, strategize, and work on your vision and mission statements. This is when you write out exactly what you want to see and desire the dream to come to fruition.

4. Pace

   The rate at which you progress is important. This is a critical component of achievement of dreams and completing your goal. Ultimately, it will take time, but fulfilling the obligation to see it through must be done on purpose and with carved-out slots. You must write this into your daily, weekly, and monthly routine.

Many feel that way until they've reached a certain level of success. But most never seem to reach a state of true satisfaction because they have not zoned in, rode the tide, and conquered the goal. Many anticipated that life will just happen. It's like something mystical is going to occur for them that will change and affect their entire scope on life.

I am indeed a lifelong learner. I already had a strong desire to "further" my education, although I hadn't finished elementary, junior high, and high school. I lined up all my stuffed animals every day and lectured them. I also tortured one of my siblings and made him one of my class participants. It was obvious even then that I loved teaching. However, after my first job experience was in a customer service role, I also thought I liked that, then I had several other roles. My journey went full circle, and I ended up coming back to my initial gut desire of teaching others.

Admittedly, I think that human beings are always searching for the "next big thing" to do or achieve in life. I would not say that "all of us" aren't content, because some are quite satisfied and have accomplished many achievements. There is always room for growth, development, and improvement, no matter what you've achieved in your life. Whether it's a professional, personal, or spiritual area in your life, no one has peaked in potential in every area.

After the conditioning occurs and the decision is made mentally to achieve your goal, then there must be a translation into physical "actions" or "activities."

In the case of world-class athletes, some have been born with natural talents and abilities, but still must have unyielding drive and commitment. Even the best athletes must hard work and sacrifice to make it to the top in their sport. It takes countless hours of practice and preparation to reach the pinnacle state. Not everyone has athletic abilities, but undeniably, everyone has some type of talent and calling in life where they should want to reach their "pinnacle" state (peak). There must be a determination to go all the way to be fulfilled in this area.

Even as I'm writing this book, it is becoming very clear to me that not only do I have the gift of writing, but there are so many other components that I want to attack that will make my efforts successful. Just by me following through on this project is sparking many ideas and dreams. One must be determined to succeed in his area of focus, regardless of any future obstacles that he or she may be facing.

Words are one of the most powerful tools we will ever possess. Words are irrefutable. They can be used as a tool and source of reference in difficult times, so that's my goal . . . to encourage you to do it now.

How long have you been waiting to see certain things fulfilled in your life? Whether it's weight loss or that big promotion or that big return on your educational investment . . . Regardless of what your chosen point of focus may be, I've learned over the years that our lives are made up of so many different compartments. Be aware that just because you may have built up yourself in one area does not mean you're that accomplished in another.

The question becomes . . . What are you going to do about it? What are you willing to do to ensure that your life does change, that you do accomplish your goals and dreams? Obviously, there is not one formula that fits all, that works for everything or every circumstance. Otherwise, I could package that pill and everyone would live happily ever after.

Procrastination is such a paralyzing behavior that once bought into, it seems that you're constantly digging a deeper, deeper hole and will never accomplish your goal. One of the greatest problems in our society today is procrastination. The phrase, "The choices we're making today will affect our tomorrow." Well, the choices you're NOT making today are STILL affecting your tomorrow.

Let's look at the idea of wanting to lose weight as an example because many of us can relate to the idea of wanting to look better and feel better about yourself. So the question then becomes, how badly do you want to look and feel better? Most have a general sense of what we would like to see, but in many cases, we are stopping ourselves. There are several factors that we'll then use as a crutch or excuse about why we can't. First, simply have a made-up mind that we're going to stay the course to see this change through in our health, but then come the excuses of *I don't have time, I'm too busy,* or how about, *I can't afford to eat right. The right foods are just too expensive for me to buy every week.* Or the excuse may be not wanting to give up those tasty food items simply because of the lack of willpower to live without certain things (i.e., the fries, sodas, or chocolate bars, etc.). Some things we feel we just can't resist or we don't want to make that sacrifice. Let's not forget this one: *I just don't have the time to work out.* Many cases, it's because something seems like it's going to be a lot of work, and there's just seemingly not enough time to do them all. It feels like "one more thing" to add to our already long list.

There are many personality types. One in particular is the individual who is willing to work his or her fingers to the bone for others, while investing little to no interest in yourself. Don't get me wrong; with everything, there has to be a balance. Have you ever witnessed an overly self-centered adult? It's all about you, all the time. That is not the way. Back to balance, then you have the people who are willing to self-sacrifice everything all the time for others, and that's not good either. Many times, women will give their very lives for their families. They are wives, mothers, daughters, sisters, counselors, breadwinners—you name it.

Regardless of your profession, personality type, or personal convictions, there is a universal question that you've asked yourself in your heart, and that question is . . . What's the next big thing for me?

There's really nothing holding you back but YOU. Now, the million-dollar question: How do you get past you? Like anything else, there must be clarity on which direction you are taking; in other words, I believe the first and foremost task is to set personal goals by establishing a mission and vision statement for yourself.

Time Waits for No One . . .

I think we're all at that stage we simply just want to see results. I know I am. How long have you been waiting to see certain things fulfilled in your life? As for me, I sometimes feel like . . . How much longer *for this?* Or, is time running out *for that?* Well, whatever is the solution, do it now. In other words, do all that you can to prepare yourself for the situation. Some type of action is required on your part. Ask yourself, are you transitioning into or out of a circumstance?

So, what's the problem with the people sitting right here on top of this gold mine (of opportunity)? I see and hear stories of people every day reaching outside of themselves and pursuing the impossible. The grass is no greener for one than the next in this land of opportunity when it comes down to the requirement of hard work. Even when you study the lives of successful people of the past and the present, the one thing that they all have in common is a strong work ethic. You can't be lazy and a dreamer. You have to be willing to work hard and be challenged if you want to achieve a certain level of success in life. It's time to do all that you can do to achieve your own success. It's time to be empowered to take ownership of your future. How would I know whether I could be a best-selling author if I never write a book? Whatever you want to be, you can work toward that goal with proper planning, time, and effort. You will never know if you don't try.

15

THE "DO"

One of the most amazing coined phrases of our time was "Just Do It." Those are three powerful words, but the most powerful of the three is "*do*." It's time to make a decision to go in the direction of your life's goals.

If your lifelong passion is to become a medical doctor, you have to weigh out the time commitment and required resources that are necessary. It's astounding how a vision can be there, but even some great visionaries don't have a clue how to move forward and execute. I think that is even more painful—to have all this bottled up inside and yet not have an outlet. The late Dr. Myles Munroe often talked about the amount of treasure that's in the graveyard. An immeasurable amount of talented individuals died before their time. Now, the other side to this is some people who don't know what to pursue and who aren't pursuing anything.

I started out as a clerk/cashier at a drugstore. Well, that led to me counting money as a bank teller; then that exposure gave me insight and interest into the business world, which led to me becoming a personal banker, which led to me working for the finance division, personally managing the accounts of some very wealthy clients, and so on. Nothing is by accident, and no skill goes wasted, in my opinion.

So that leads me to my first main point: You must educate yourself, both figuratively and literally. I believe even if you are unclear initially on what you want to do as a profession, a good education leads you to those answers. Textbooks, classroom interactions, people you meet, field trips, those will all eventually lead you to that "aha!" moment. In some cases, educating yourself simply means that in its literal sense.

My father was a genius. I mean, whatever he wanted to learn, he simply got the materials, studied it extensively, and did it. From laying tile to fixing cars to budgeting, he knew how to do it all without a high school diploma (which he did earn later in his life). He had such a driven focus that whenever he was set on doing something, he would let nothing hinder him . . . ever.

Success Starts with a Decision

Success starts with a decision. But in order to know and achieve success, one must know clearly and define the definition of success for his or her life.

Success can look completely different for everyone. Our lives are comprised of a number of different things. Our upbringing and our choices seem to have the most lasting impact because none of us had any control of the families we've been birthed into or their experiences regarding child rearing.

Success may be rated by the number of zeros at the end of your bank account, whereas someone else may consider being able to pay their rent and buy food for their family an accomplishment. What these examples propose to me is that success is relative; it differs for each individual.

People have different paths in life. As children, of course, our paths are based on the circumstances in which we were raised, which is completely out of our control. Some children know what they want to be when they grow up; they seek that path, and they never look back. There are others, like me, who have glimpses of what they want to do, but it was a bit more of a struggle to narrow it down. The great news is your life does not have to be placed in a box. And if you decide to make a change in your career now that you've explored and "seen the light," so to speak, it's quite okay.

It's all right to realize, and I think we all must, that life is a journey and will change at different intervals. A simple visual is that of one who has now matured and crossed over to a more senior status in age and capabilities. Logically, you are no longer seeking to do what you did in your younger years, and in most instances, you are no longer capable of doing that anyway. Your entire outlook on the world has completely shifted.

Die Trying

The biggest obstacle, for the most part, is the lack of faith or confidence one may have in his or her abilities.

How hard are you really willing to work for what you want? There is no reward without sacrifice, pursuit, or challenge. The scriptures even tell us "faith without works is dead"; in other words, you can talk a good game and dream big; however, some have described that faith without works is hallucinations.

16

BELIEVE IN YOURSELF, ONLY BELIEVE

The first thing I would say is that truth is acceptance. Truth is the understanding that I must accept the reality of today, and knowing this, I can start the change I want for tomorrow.

The definition of *believe* is to accept (something) as true; feel sure of the truth of. You have to first believe in you. You must accept the truth of all of you.

I am all for the concept of having supporters and mentors because we all can learn from someone else (at least, something). The worst thing in the world is not to be able to see yourself out of the proper lens.

I've noticed that individuals sometimes tend to have the hardest time accepting that they are the reason or root cause of why certain things have not occurred or been accomplished their lives. *We* are the root of what needs a change. Having been in the field of education,

I've met with parents to talk about their children's academic capabilities or behavior challenges. Sometimes parents get offended when you have to point out something that benefits their child, if corrected. They seem to take it personally. I think they *should* take it personally, but in a more diplomatic fashion, not an accusatory one. They may make excuses or be tempted to blame others. Needless to say, whichever occurs, it does not help determine how to best serve the needs of the child.

Now this leads to my example of having been an educator and striving to work with parents and their children to bring information, and, hopefully, seek a better outcome. I've observed how challenging it can be for parents to see the need to provoke change in their own lives when it comes down to what they are doing to support their children's learning. Parents are truly their child's first teacher.

It's so important to surround yourself by those that believe in you, people you hold in high esteem who can encourage you to not only be your best, but who are also willing to tell you the things you may not want to hear, which is the truth. Sometimes facing the truth will hurt, but it may also be the stimulus for the change you need. I can support you, listen to you, and consider you, even though I may have to impart what you may not agree with.

I am all for the concept of having supporters and mentors because everyone can learn from someone else. Every person that comes in your path, no matter how big or small, comes from a story.

It boils down to you making a conscious decision that this is something you're going to do and will strive to do consistently. People may have disappointed us many times over. But you also must be willing to extend what you want to receive. There are sometimes people who we don't connect with. Maybe it can be a simple lack of communication that's causing the despair. Learn to believe in others on the journey of believing in yourself.

Brand Trials: Challenges Will Come

Trials and challenges of life can sometimes make us or break us. These are the situations that begin to mold and shape us into another person. For example, if you become seriously ill and go through the process of hospitalization, surgery, and ultimately, recovery, you can now relate to someone who's had that same experience. So if it didn't leave you down and out and you chose to view the experience in another light, then be thankful for having survived your circumstances. You now have the opportunity to see others differently because you've had that experience and you now know how it made you feel. You can now choose to become a more compassionate and caring person when relating to those who are ill.

When I lived through my first layoff, I really felt the heat and was very anxious about just moving to another department. I tried and tried, but it seemed that every door was closed in my face. And lo and behold, just through a conversation with my father, the lightbulb turned on. Maybe this was a strategic time to move on and to consider all of my options, even that of a possible career change.

So although I had established my skills, up to this point in the business industry, it was now time to reestablish myself in an entirely different sector. Sometimes the changes you must make are so drastic, they require a major leap of faith. Yes, it was the time to consider something I had pondered in my college career days. Making a career change after much soul-searching and prayer was the best career move I could have ever made at that time.

Change isn't always an easy thing, but change is necessary, as previously mentioned. One must always take into account that any type of change will affect the makeup of our brand, both on the inside and on the outside. Most changes always start from within.

No matter the profession, there are transferable skill sets that deeply impact our brand. For example, showing kindness, remaining respectful, and great communication are just a few that come to mind. No matter if you are a politician or a priest, these are important skills. Remain positive and not negative, and keep an attitude of gratitude. Self-examination, or a state of reflection, is becoming a general practice for many types of professions and work settings, whether you own your business or are working for someone else. It's imperative to find balance in your life no matter what the profession.

A Brand-new Start: It's Never too Late to Make a Change

The point that I want to emphasize in this chapter is that it's never too late to make the necessary changes to increase your brand. Brand awareness is the ability to improve the representation of *who you are*. Brand awareness is the establishment of how you are perceived, and it helps others to establish your perception in life.

Everyone is known for something in our personality, our individuality. There is a uniqueness that we carry among the masses. Have you ever seen an instance in the media where you have two celebrities who somehow end up wearing the exact same outfit at a particular function and they have been caught on camera by the paparazzi? Next thing you know, they pop up in a magazine or online in a fashion section with the caption, "Who wore it best?" Comments from everyone around the world flood in. This is a great example of perception, because the feedback is probably tied to having history or prior knowledge of that celebrity.

Some may have more familiarity of one celebrity's work over another's, and they then make their comments based on this factor. Another responder may have no prior knowledge of either celebrity and are simply incorporating their own sense of style in the opinion poll. Some may be trained skilled fashion bloggers who are familiar with the "official" world of fashion and can tell us what's in and what's not based on global thinking. There are a number of factors that play into perception.

As we dig deeper into this example, what if you have one person in the photo who may appear heavier than the other. If you have a bias about people that are overweight, it will definitely tie in to your decision. But on the flip side, if you were familiar with that person and felt they connected with you and had a great personality, maybe you will be more favorable to that individual.

Right now, the accessibility to technological resources is becoming outdated as I write. The technologists of the world are constantly coming up with the next big thing. They're making things quicker and thinner and savvier. For example, the smartphone is not just a phone; it's many things wrapped up in one. It's a video camera, digital camera, personal assistant, alarm, flashlight, etc. The applications are also limitless, it seems, when it comes to its capabilities. I feel like, after an entire year of my latest phone purchase, I have barely touched the surface of what it can really do. I am always learning something new that the phone can do.

The aspect of being on the potter's wheel signifies that the potter has the responsibility to actually shape the clay into the vessel he desires it to be. There are times when excess clay is removed to get it into the desired shape. Because of consistently striving to become better, it's a great analogy to consider. So, change is a big part of the branding process.

There is something about the uniqueness of every individual that, regardless of their outward exterior, who they are inside takes precedence and brings a sense of style to who you are in general. I'm not necessarily referring to style just in the sense of fashion, although fashion does definitely have a place in my descriptor. But I am referring to more of the inner you, your aura; and that thing in you will eventually shine forth.